THE CRAPPIE BOOK
BASICS AND BEYOND

KEITH SUTTON

STOEGER PUBLISHING COMPANY
is a division of Benelli USA

Benelli USA
Vice President and General Manager:
  Stephen Otway
Vice President of Marketing and Communications:
  Stephen McKelvain

Stoeger Publishing Company
President: Jeffrey Reh
Publisher: Jennifer Thomas
Managing Editor: Harris J. Andrews
Creative Director: Cynthia T. Richardson
Graphic Designer: William Graves
Special Accounts Manager: Julie Brownlee
Publishing Assistant: Stacy Logue
Layout & Design: William Graves
Illustrations: William Graves
Proofreader: Amy Jones

© 2006 by Keith Sutton
All rights reserved.

No part of this book may be reproduced or transmitted in any form or by any means, electronic or mechanical, including photocopying, recording, or by any information storage and retrieval system, without permission in writing from the Publisher.

Published 2006, 2007 by:
Stoeger Publishing Company
17603 Indian Head Highway, Suite 200
Accokeek, Maryland 20607

BK0513
ISBN-13: 978-0-88317-219-9
ISBN-10: 0-88317-291-7
Library of Congress Control Number:
  2004109588

Manufactured in the United States of America.

Distributed to the book trade and
to the sporting goods trade by:
Stoeger Industries
17603 Indian Head Highway, Suite 200
Accokeek, Maryland 20607
301 283-6100 Fax: 301 283-6986
www.stoegerpublishing.com

OTHER PUBLICATIONS:
Shooter's Bible
  The World's Standard
  Firearms Reference Book
Gun Trader's Guide
  Complete Fully Illustrated
  Guide to Modern Firearms
  with Current Market Values

Hunting & Shooting:
Archer's Bible Presents:
  The Bowhunter's Guide
Deer Rifles & Cartridges
Elk Hunter's Bible
High Performance
  Muzzleloading
  Big Game Rifles
High Power Rifle Accuracy
Hunt Club
  Management Guide
The Hunter's Journal
Hunting Tough Bucks
Hunting Whitetails
  East & West
Hunting the Whitetail Rut
Modern Shotgunning
Shotgunning for Deer
Sure-Fire Whitetail Tactics
Taxidermy Guide
Trailing the Hunter's Moon
Whitetail Strategies

Firearms:
Antique Guns:
  A Collector's Guide
Beretta Pistols:
  The Ultimate Guide
Firearms Disassembly
  with Exploded Views
Guns & Ammo: The Shooter's
  Guide to Classic Firearms
Gunsmithing Made Easy
How to Buy & Sell Used Guns
Model 1911: Automatic Pistol
Modern Beretta Firearms
Successful Gun Trading

Reloading:
The Handloader's Manual of
  Cartridge Conversions 3rd Ed.

Fishing:
Archer's Bible Presents:
  Practical Bowfishing
Big Bass Zone
Catfishing:
  Beyond the Basics
Fishing Made Easy
Fishing Online:
  1,000 Best Web Sites
Flyfishing for Trout A-Z
Out There Fishing
Walleye Pro's Notebook

Cooking Game:
The Complete Book of
  Dutch Oven Cooking
Dress 'Em Out
Wild About Freshwater Fish
Wild About Game Birds
Wild About Seafood
Wild About Venison
Wild About Waterfowl
World's Best Catfish Cookbook

Nature:
U.S. Guide to Venomous
  Snakes and Their Mimics

Pocket Guides:
The Pocket
  Deer Hunting Guide
The Pocket
  Disaster Survival Guide
The Pocket
  First-Aid Field Guide
The Pocket
  Fishing Basics Guide
The Pocket
  Outdoor Survival Guide

Fiction:
The Hunt
Wounded Moon

Nonfiction:
Escape In Iraq:
  The Thomas Hamill Story

PHOTO CREDITS:
Matt Sutton: *5*; Duane Raver, USFWS: *11, 66*;
Jack Bissell: *101*; Zach Sutton: *177-181*

CONTENTS

INTRODUCTION 5

Chapter I: GETTING TO KNOW CRAPPIE
Crappie Basics 6
12 Places You'll Always Find Crappie 14

Chapter II: TACKLE TIPS
Poles 20
Rods & Reels 24
How to Stuff a Crappie Tackle Box 28

Chapter III: LURE SELECTION
Pick the Perfect Jig 34
Spinners for Crappie 43
Crankbait Crappie 48
Secret Weapon: Lipless Crankbaits 51
Pumping Iron: Catching Crappie on Spoons 56
Heavy Metal: Bladebaits & Tailspinners 59

Chapter IV: CONSIDERING BAIT
Crappie Fishing With Minnows 64
Overlooked Crappie Catchers 73

Chapter V: CRAPPIE SEASONS

SPRING	Crappie on the Beds	78
	River Tactics for the Spawn	82
	Sight-Fishing for Spring Slabs	87
	Spring Fishing Tips	92
SUMMER	Dog Days Fillets	96
	Crappie at Night	100
	Summer Fishing Tips	106
FALL	Understanding Fall Transition	110
	Fall Fishing Tips	117
WINTER	Ice-Box Slabs	121
	Christmas Tree Crappie	125
	Winter Fishing Tips	132

Chapter VI: TACTICAL TIPS
Trolling for Crappie 136
A Lesson on Super-Structure 142
Understanding Oxbows 148
Hideaway Crappie 154
Overlooked Crappie Fishing Methods 160

Chapter VII: TROPHY TACTICS
One Guide's Secrets for Giant Crappie 164
Tips for Catching Trophy Crappie 172

Chapter VIII: CLEANING & COOKING CRAPPIE
How to Pan-Dress & Fillet a Crappie 176
Crappie Recipes 182

INDEX 192

INTRODUCTION

Many books have been written about crappie fishing. I'm a fan of every one I've ever read, and to be quite honest, the folks who wrote those books—people like Steve Wunderle, Tim Huffman, Jim Robbins, Larry Larsen, Horace Carter, Bill Dance and Charlie Brewer—know more about crappie fishing than I'll ever learn.

That being the case, you might wonder why I've written yet another treatise about fishing for America's favorite panfish.

First of all, this book is a labor of love. I enjoy fishing for every kind of fish that's likely to take a bait or strike a lure. Crappie, however, rank near the top on my list of favorites. I started fishing for them at age six and immediately fell in love with these calico sunfish. That love has never diminished. Put me on a backcountry crappie lake with a cane pole and a few minnows and jigs, and I'm as happy as a man can be. Being a writer, it's only natural I should want to share my thoughts about something I enjoy so much.

Second, I believe I have some unique insights on the sport that are worth sharing. You'll find a lot of basic information on these pages, for sure. You'll learn about crappie biology, the types of structure and cover to fish, how to select and use basic crappie-catchers such as jigs and minnows, and tried-and-true tactics for catching crappie throughout the seasons. But you'll also discover many new and innovative ways of finding and catching crappie. I've been fortunate to fish with some of the country's finest crappie fishermen, and more fortunate still that they've been willing to share so much of their knowledge. You'll find their insights transformed into text on the pages inside. I've also spent a lifetime studying crappie behavior in the lakes and rivers I fish, and the things I've discovered first-hand provide the basis for much of the information here.

I hope you enjoy this labor of love. I hope you learn many new things as you delve into the pages that follow. Most of all, I hope all your crappie fishing adventures are fruitful and create memories that will last a lifetime.

--Keith Sutton

Chapter 1

GETTING TO KNOW CRAPPIE

Crappie Basics

Its strike is often so delicate, it may be hooked before you know it. Seldom will one weighing over a pound or two be caught. It puts up an admirable tussle on light tackle, but it's not really a hard fighter. So why is the crappie such a popular gamefish?

There's no single answer. Anglers laud the crappie for a combination of characteristics that make crappie fishing pure fun.

Crappie are found in hundreds of thousands of lakes and streams through the U.S. In-the-know anglers haul them in spring, summer, autumn and winter. Anything these sunfish lack in size, they compensate for with sheer numbers and the ease with which they are caught.

Crappie rank high among America's favorite sport fish. Almost 7 million anglers fish for them each year.

Fancy equipment? No need. It doesn't matter if you use an old cane pole or a $200 ultralight rig. Both catch crappie.

Good eating? Absolutely. Crappie have flaky, white meat suitable for a variety of recipes. Nothing is finer than crappie fillets properly prepared and cooked.

Crappie are fish for kids of all ages. Sure, trout are bedazzling jumpers. Catfish are superb dinner fare. And stripers are brutal battlers. For many anglers, however, crappie are the favorites because the certainty of some kind of fishing action is far better than promised battles that never come.

The Difference Between Black and White

The world has only two species of crappie—the black crappie (*Pomoxis nigromaculatus*) and the white crappie (*Pomoxis annularis*), both found exclusively in North America. They belong to the sunfish family, *Centrarchidae*, which also includes largemouth bass, bluegills and other popular warm water gamefish.

Anglers seldom bother to distinguish between black and white crappie. Both are uniquely beautiful panfish with large, showy fins and metallic bodies that glisten like silver ingots. Fishing techniques are identical for each. Neither is more worthy quarry

The differences between a white crappie (top) and black crappie (bottom) are minor, but most avid crappie anglers can readily distinguish one species from the other.

than the other. But if you catch a crappie big enough for the record books, it must be positively identified as one or the other.

The most reliable method of separating the two is counting the dorsal fin spines. Black crappie normally have seven or eight; whites usually have six, but sometimes five.

Color is not as dependable, but white crappie are paler, and dark spots on the sides usually are arranged in regular vertical bars. Black crappie are typically darker and have irregular spotting.

Black crappie fare best over a firm bottom in relatively cool, clear water, and they strongly relate to aquatic vegetation. They're slightly fussier about their environment than white crappie, which flourish in warmer, siltier waters that often have soft substrates.

Some lakes and streams have populations of only one species. Over a great portion of their respective ranges, however, the two can be found together in the same waters.

Most sage crappie anglers couldn't care less one way or the other. They're after crappie, plain and simple. And the type of crappie that is caught doesn't matter one iota.

Range

Black crappie originally were found in the eastern half of the United States except for the northeastern seaboard. The range of this species was greatly expanded, however, by introductions into eastern sections of the country where it wasn't found originally, and throughout the much of the West and Midwest. Washington received its first stockings in 1890, California in 1891, Idaho in 1892 and Oregon in 1893.

The original range of the white crappie extended from eastern South Dakota to New York, then south to Alabama and Texas. This species also has been widely introduced into new waters, and like the black crappie, it now is found in all lower 48 states. It tends to be more at home in the oxbows, large lakes and sluggish rivers of the South, while the black crappie, which thrives best in colder, clearer water, can be found as far north as southern Canada.

Crappie also have been stocked in Mexico and Panama, with populations thriving in both countries.

Size

Average size depends on local conditions. One-half- to 1-pound crappie comprise the usual catch in most waters, but prime lakes and rivers often yield "barn-doors" in the 2- to 3-pound class.

Black crappie growth is generally slower than that of the white crappie, but because it has a stockier body, a black crappie of a given length generally will weigh more than a white crappie of the same length. For example, a 12-inch black crappie will be heavier than a 12-inch white crappie.

The two primary record-keeping organizations—the International Game Fish Association and the National Fresh Water Fishing Hall of Fame—both recognize a 5-pound, 3-ounce white crappie caught in Enid Lake, Mississippi in 1957 as the all-tackle world record. However, the organizations differ in the record listings when it comes to black crappie. The IGFA shows a tie between two 4-pound, 8-ounce fish, one caught in Kerr Lake, Virginia in 1981, and another caught in Otoe County, Nebraska in 2003. The Hall of Fame's top white crappie is a 6-pounder taken from Westwego Canal, Louisiana (a backwater of the Mississippi River) in 1969.

The Hall of Fame also shows an all-tackle record for the hybrid crappie, a cross between a black and white crappie. That 2-pound, 1-ounce specimen was caught in Lake Elizabeth, Wisconsin in 1988.

Food Habits

Crappie feed primarily on small fishes, aquatic insects and tiny crustaceans. The proportions of these food items vary with locality, season and the crappie's age. Young crappie feed more on small crustaceans. Adults subsist mainly on fish, with insects also making up a small percentage of the diet. Small shad are the principle food item for adult crappie in many reservoirs.

Biologists studying crappie in Arkansas' Beaver Lake found that adult black crappie tend to eat more insects in spring and fishes in other seasons, while adult white crappie eat fishes year-round. The researchers believe these food habits eventually caused white crappie to become more abundant in the reservoir than the previously dominant black crappie. As the lake aged, there was an apparent reduction in the number of insects important to black crappie, so the numbers of black crappie fell, and white crappie became the dominant species.

What's in a Name?

The word crappie has its roots in the Canadian-French word *crapet*, which was an early name for the species. *Crapet* probably is derived from the French *crêpe*, a pancake, in reference to the fish's general shape.

In some areas, the name crappie has taken on a most indelicate pronunciation, similar to the dice game craps. Most people, however, pronounce it croppie, which is more in keeping with the word's derivation.

For many years, fish reference books referred to the white crappie simply as crappie, and the black crappie was known as the calico bass.

Crappie have more aliases than a most-wanted criminal, over 50 in all. Among the most commonly heard today are speck, speckled perch, white perch, calico, papermouth (in reference to the crappie's delicate mouth parts) and sac-a-lait (Cajun-French for "bag of milk"). More archaic nicknames include gold ring (for the ring around the pupil of the eye), bachelor perch, banklick, chinquapin, lamplight, tinmouth, strawberry bass, silver perch, barfish, bridge perch, John Demon, timber crappie, Mason perch, straw bass, bitterhead, goggle-eye, shad, grass bass, newlight and Campbellite.

The latter name, Campbellite, was mentioned in an 1878 biennial report by the Kansas State Board of Agriculture, which said, "[The crappie's] slang name in the West used to be the 'Campbellite,' because it made its first appearance in the tributaries of the Ohio about the time Alexander Campbell first began to achieve a reputation." Campbell was a religious leader of the early 1820s whose followers performed full-immersion baptisms and sometimes were referred to as Campbellites, New Light Christians or simply New Lights, the latter being another strange vernacular name associated with the crappie.

To avoid confusion caused by such a plethora of common names, scientific names are used. The black crappie's is *Pomoxis nigromaculatus*; the white crappie's is *Pomoxis annularis*. *Pomoxis* means sharp opercle, referring to the spiny, pointed rear edge of the gill cover. Nigromaculatus is Latin for "black spotted." *Annularis* is Latin for "having rings," a reference to the dark vertical bands along the sides of the white crappie.

Black Crappie

White Crappie

Reproduction

The fact that black crappie and white crappie select different spawning habitats is part of the reason they remain two distinct species. In some man-made lakes, however, the two crappie species sometimes overlap in their habitat and they hybridize. The hybrids are sometimes called, appropriately enough, "gray crappie." And they may be more abundant in some waters than many people would suspect. A study on Alabama's Weiss Lake, for example, determined that 18 percent of the population were hybrids and another three percent was offspring from hybrid parents.

Crappie move to shallows to nest in spring when the water temperature nears 56 degrees. That might be January in Florida and July in northern Ohio.

Adult males of both species undergo a noticeable color change as the season begins. Their cheeks and belly become considerably darker, and the upper sides often take on a brassy hue.

The males build the nests, using their tails to fan silt away from a bottom area composed of fine gravel or finely divided plant roots, often near a log or other large object. The nests almost invariably are in shallow coves protected from wave action, and there may be many nests in a single cove. The depth at which nests are found can vary considerably, from less than one foot to as much as 20 feet.

A large female may lay as many as 180,000 eggs. Spawning with several males is common, and each female may produce eggs several times during the spawning period.

The eggs hatch in two to four days, and the fry remain in the nest several days where they are guarded by the male.

When crappie reach the second or third summer of life, they are sexually mature and will spawn the following spring. The maximum life span is about seven or eight years, although few crappie live beyond age three or four.

Seasonal Behavior

Understanding the general seasonal habits of crappie is important so you can locate prime crappie fishing areas year-round.

Summer and winter crappie typically form large, loose schools and usually hold near cover in 10 to 35 feet of water. In oxbows, look for fish near old river channels or the basin of the lake. Reservoir fish may concentrate in deep timber near channel breaks or humps. River crappie tend to hole up in deep backwaters. Using a sonar fish finder makes the difficult job of locating these fish much simpler.

In spring, as the water temperature climbs into the upper 50s and low 60s, crappie move to their spawning grounds, usually in shallow, wind-protected coves with good cover. Most anglers find crappie near shoreline cover—button willows, cypress trees, blowdowns, stickups and weedbeds. Larger crappie may be farther out over shallow, main-lake humps or near channel edges adjacent to shallow flats.

During cold fronts, crappie may leave shallows for deeper water. Deep timber along channel edges or underwater humps is a favorite retreat. The more severe the front, the deeper the fish withdraw.

Locating autumn crappie is especially hard. Fish in 8-foot depths one day may move to 20 feet the next. They may hold over brushpiles in the morning and move to deep points by evening. The best advice this season is keep moving until you find feeding fish.

Blacknose Crappie

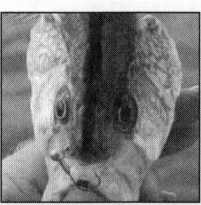

In many waters, anglers catch crappie that have a dark brown or black stripe running under the chin, over the nose and across part of the back. These beautifully marked fish, often considered a special prize for the crappie fan, are called "blacknose crappie."

Several stories have been propagated to explain the origins of these fish. Most folks believe they are hybrid fish, a cross between black crappie and white crappie. Others believe they are juvenile crappie that will lose the black stripe with age.

In fact, blacknose crappie are simply an unusual color strain of the black crappie. They were first described in Ohio in 1957. A later study reported they had been found in 13 states. One of those states was Arkansas, where blacknose crappie turned up in Beaver and Bull Shoals lakes. Some of those fish were transported to an Arkansas state fish hatchery in the 1960s, where biologists learned how to propagate the strain and produce blacknose crappie by design rather than accident. This distinctive crappie is now being raised in state fish hatcheries for stocking public fishing waters throughout the country. Because the blacknose is easily recognized even by untrained observers, it has proven valuable for studying crappie management strategies in lakes where it has been introduced.

Working jigs or other small lures in and around the flooded sticks of beaver lodges is a good way to zero in on crappie.

12 Places You'll Always Find Crappie

Lakes and rivers contain many crappie hotspots. If you're lucky, you can pick a spot at random, cast your bait and start reeling in slabs. But most of us aren't so lucky. For consistent success, especially on unfamiliar waters, we need more information; we need to know where, specifically, hungry crappie are likely to be.

Some places are definitely better than others, including the following 12 places where crappie gather like kids around an ice-cream truck, gobbling every morsel that passes by.

Points

Points are excellent crappie hotspots year-round because they serve as pathways for fish moving back and forth between shallow and deep water. By working a point methodically from near-shore to offshore, you should be able to determine the day's depth pattern and use it to find crappie on other points or structural features.

Work a jig or minnow around all visible cover and fish-concentrating structure—stumps, fallen and standing timber, rocks, man-made brush piles and the like. If most crappie are caught around features at the point's upper end, then concentrate on shallow features when you move to other areas. Likewise, if crappie seem to be favoring deeper areas on the point, you should continue fishing deep-water structure until you notice a shift in the pattern.

Shallow Ledges & Channel Breaks

Crappie anglers should always watch their sonar unit for signs of shallow ledges and channel breaks beneath the water. These aren't the deep drop-offs that fall away for 10 feet or more along a major river channel, but rather shallow ditches, cuts, ledges and gullies that are often found near bankside bluffs or close to coves and bays. These structures are especially productive when associated with nearby weed-beds, timber stands or other suitable crappie cover.

Fish Shelters

Fisheries agencies often construct elaborate fish shelters by sinking reefs of trees and brush in waters where lack of fish cover has limited fish production. Buoys mark the locations of most shelters. Others are marked on maps and can be pinpointed using sonar. All such shelters are likely to harbor crappie concentrations year-round.

Beaver Lodges

Crappie love beaver lodges, often hiding in the dense woody tangles created when beavers lay sticks to build a home. Because this type of cover is so dense, you'll probably have to work it with a jig and jigging pole. Start shallow, and fish your way to the outer edges of the lodge. Some crappie will be in shallow cover, but most big crappie will be on the outer edges where the sticks disappear into deeper water.

Offshore cypress trees are always worth checking for crappie.

Flooded Willows

When fishing big rivers and their backwaters, you can bet your bottom dollar you'll always find crappie holding around inundated willow trees. Fishing the outermost willows in these areas is the best way to catch lots of big crappie, but if that fails to produce, work other portions of the willow stand. Be attentive, too, for long rows of flooded willows on natural lakes where overflows raise the water level. These are hotspots not to be missed.

Inundated Lakes and Ponds

Small ponds and lakes inundated when larger lakes fill are prime locales for crappie year-round. These offer easy access to deep-water holding areas and shallow feeding spots. They're especially productive in large shallow lakes.

Pinpoint the spot with sonar, then look within it for points, drop-offs, sunken islands or humps that attract crappie. If scattered trees or stumps exist around the perimeter, fish them carefully.

Threadfin Shad Schools

Threadfin shad schools are almost always followed by loose groups of big crappie, and sometimes schools of smaller fish. When the body of water you're fishing is inhabited by threadfins (check with the local fisheries department or knowledgeable anglers), watch for clues to help you pinpoint the baitfish.

Did You Know?

 In 1993, Louisiana became the first and only state to designate the crappie (in this case, the white crappie) as its official state fish.

 Several places lay claim to the title "Crappie Capital of the World," including Weiss Lake, Alabama; Kentucky Lake in Kentucky and Tennessee; Grand Lake, Oklahoma; and Lake Okeechobee, Florida.

As a general rule, look for shad schools in deeper water throughout winter and around midday during warm seasons. Look in shallower water near dawn and dusk in spring, summer and fall. You may see shad leaping or swirling as predator fish chase them. On a fish finder, a school of threadfins usually will appear as a band of pixels one to several feet thick. Crappie will appear as scattered individuals around or beneath the shad, seldom more than half a dozen or so together. Find them and you can target them with appropriate lures.

Cypress Trees

Crappie gather round bald cypresses wherever these water-loving trees are found. They won't be found around the same trees year-round, however. When the spring spawn is underway, you'll find more crappie by fishing cypresses in shallow shoreline waters. In summer and winter, you'll do better fishing trees standing in or near deeper water. Autumn may find crappie deep or shallow, so fish cypress trees in a variety of places, deep and shallow.

In waters with hundreds of cypresses, it helps to narrow the scope of your search to particular types of trees. Cypress trees standing alone or in small clusters offshore often indicate the presence of an underwater hump (a favorite crappie haunt) and always are worth trying. Trees with big open hollows also should be checked as big crappie love to hide in the dark interiors to ambush prey fish passing by. Also focus your attention on the outermost cypress trees on points, trees with lots of tall knees erupting from the water some distance from the buttressed trunk and big cypress stumps with hollow interiors.

Crappie anglers often find their quarry holding near isolated bits of cover and structure such as this stump in open water.

Isolated Stumps

You'll rarely go wrong working a jig or minnow around a stump that is isolated from other types of structure. If you can find an area with lots of widely scattered stumps, so much the better. Fish each stump thoroughly on all sides, targeting the shady side first on sunny days.

The best stumps often are those barely visible beneath the water's surface, but you'll have to move

Studying a bottom contour map of the body of water you plan to fish helps you pinpoint structures where crappie are likely to be.

slowly and watch carefully to find them. Anglers often carry short lengths of cane to stick in the tops of such stumps as markers. It's then easier to come back and fish the stumps throughout the day.

Inflow Water-Control Structures

Many crappie waters have water-control structures that bring an inflow of fresh water to the main water body. This may be a pipe jutting from a bank with water pouring out the end, an underwater well head that creates a boil in an otherwise calm surface or a big culvert with a fresh inflow of rain after a shower. Baitfish such as shad gather in the well-oxygenated water around these structures, and crappie gather to eat the baitfish. Working spinners and spoons through these areas is often very productive.

Thicket Structures

In waters where the edges of good crappie cover get pounded by scores of anglers, the biggest crappie often move inside dense cover stands (thickets) to avoid the ruckus. For example, if a lake has acres of button willows, slabs rarely are caught along the easily reached edges of this emergent vegetation. To find them, pull your boat into the thicket and target particular structures within that attract crappie. This may be log or stump, the edge of a creek channel or perhaps a cluster of standing snags. Any structure different from the norm is likely to attract crappie.

When trophy crappie are your target, don't overlook these hotspots regardless of the time of year. They're difficult to reach and difficult to fish, but a jig or minnow dropped inside one of these thicket structures will nearly always entice a slab.

Humps

Locating an underwater hump is like finding a map to buried treasure for the crappie fan. These structures are among the most productive crappie spots in any lake year-round.

A bottom-contour map helps in finding humps. Look in areas near old river channels and large feeder creeks for concentric rings of contour lines. If the depth numbers grow progressively smaller when moving toward the center of the circles, it's a hump. If the depth grows larger, you've found a depression, and it, too, may be worth investigating.

When you've pinpointed the hump with sonar, learn all you can about it—its size, the steepness of drops on each side, existing cover and so forth. Narrow your fishing area to a few choice zones—points, pockets, rock beds, timbered or brushy areas, etc.—then mark them with buoys or triangulate using shoreline objects.

The best humps are five to 20 feet from the surface and have substantial deep water around them, such as a creek channel running alongside. Humps with timber, brush, rocks or other cover also are productive.

We've discussed only 12 hotspots; there are dozens more. What's important to remember is this: the best bait and equipment are useless unless hungry crappie are nearby. If you take time to find the best areas, and present your bait in the right manner, the odds improve for catching lots of crappie.

Bonus Hotspot: Channels to Backwaters

On big bottomland rivers with adjacent backwater areas, the channel connecting the two can be a great crappie magnet, especially when the channel has some current. Focus your efforts on backwater channels that are at least five feet deep, have cover such as stumps and fallen trees, and lead to a backwater that has deep enough water to attract feeding crappie.

Although you can find crappie in these channels year-round, the best fishing time is just after the spawn when hungry fish are moving out of the backwaters, or during a slow rise or fall of the main river.

Pickups in Stickups

One tactic that may help you pinpoint crappie is fishing gradually sloping, stickup-covered flats in 10-20 feet of water near channel breaks. These areas provide crappie the security of deep water nearby, and when the fish want to hang around in mid-depths, they can still move vertically in the water column while relating to the woody cover. On some days, they'll suspend; other times, they'll be near the top of a stickup, or closer to its bottom. One day they'll be closer to the channel break; the next might find them on the flat's shallowest edge. Whatever the case, you've narrowed the scope of your search somewhat, and by working various portions of the flat using baits most suited to the depth you're searching, you eventually should get some pickups in the stickups.

 Chapter II

TACKLE TIPS

Poles

Fishing with long cane poles or jigging poles will often produce more fish per unit of effort than fishing with spinning or spincast tackle, especially when fishing heavy cover where casting is next to impossible.

Cane was the preferred long pole material for many years, and cane poles are still standard crappie fishing tackle nationwide. Some excellent jigging poles manufactured with modern materials have evolved, however, and taken away much of the cane market. These are much more durable and offer better "feel." They are superb for working jigs and other small lures in hard-to-reach spots.

Most jigging poles are made of fiberglass, graphite or graph-

Cane poles aren't as popular as they once were, but these natural fishing poles are still used by many crappie anglers.

ite composites. Fiberglass is more durable than graphite but lacks graphite's remarkable sensitivity. It is also heavier and bends more easily with the same amount of pull. Graphite is lighter and stiffer, and is more expensive than fiberglass. Graphite/fiberglass composites offer the best of both worlds; strength, sensitivity, flexibility and moderate pricing.

Some jigging poles have a reel built into the butt, with the line run through the inside of the pole and out the tip. Dismantling and reassembling the rig when line gets short or tangled behind the reel seat can be difficult, though. The best choice for most anglers is a pole outfitted with an ultralight underspin reel or a small line holder. These can be taped to the pole if a reel seat is not provided. They are easily spooled with the proper line size, and line still can be adjusted to suit fishing conditions.

Jigging poles vary from 8- to 20-feet long, but the longest poles are often too heavy and awkward for comfortable use. A light, limber 10- to 12-foot pole is usually the best model for catching crappie in brushy hideaways.

Long poles are important crappie-angling tools, useful for fishing open water, dense cover and everything in between.

Pole Tips

- Carry crappie poles in a variety of sizes, long and short, for use in different situations. For example, a 10-foot pole may work best when jigging around cover in water that has become stained after a rain, but if the water is clear and crappie seem persnickety, you may do better using a 14-foot pole that allows you to fish from a greater distance.
- Crappie poles often come in telescoping models, with sections that slide one inside the other to reduce the original length. These may be better than one-piece or two-piece poles when travel space is at a premium.
- Replacement tips often are available for crappie poles that have line guides. Keep a few in your tackle box along with some glue to make on-the-water repairs.
- Crappie poles that have slide rings for seating the reel allow you to move the reel up or down the handle to a spot that provides more balance. After the rings are properly positioned, they can be taped in place.
- When fishing from shore, a longer pole may be more advantageous for fishing nearby hotspots. Longer poles allow you to fish your bait or lure vertically from a greater distance so you get fewer snags.
- If you want better line control when pole fishing, your line should be about the same length as the pole to which you attach it.

Pro Tip

"Four tips can help your long-pole jigging for crappie. First, use a sensitive graphite pole because you will feel more bites and therefore catch more fish. Two, use a high-visibility line. You will get as many bites as on clear line but you will see more bites when your line twitches or moves sideways. Three, paint a one-inch color band near the tip of your pole. For example, if your pole is dark, use fluorescent white or yellow paint. The contrast will make seeing the tip easier when the sun is reflecting brightly off the water or at dusk when you have the tip shoved into the dark reaches of a bush. Four, keep your rod tip near the water for better bait control and to keep the wind from swaying your line."

--Tim Huffman, www.monstercrappie.com

Crappie anglers often opt for a light spinning combo, which allows longer casts with light lures.

Rods & Reels

Choosing a rod and reel combo for crappie fishing is like buying a vehicle. Hundreds of styles and combinations are available, everything from simple, inexpensive models to top-of-the-line imports with lots of bells and whistles. Not every angler needs or wants the same thing.

Before you buy, consider these facts.

Rods

Two of the most important considerations when selecting a rod are the power rating (ultralight, light, medium, etc.) and the action (fast, medium, slow).

When considering power, remember that ultralight rods are best for line weights of 1- to 4-pound test, and lures weighing $\frac{1}{64}$- to $\frac{1}{16}$- ounce. Light rods are best for line weights of 4- to 8 pound test and lures weighing $\frac{1}{32}$- to $\frac{1}{8}$-ounce. These two types are used by most crappie anglers who fish with a rod and reel, although medium-weight rods (for lines of 4- to 12-pound test and lures weighing $\frac{1}{8}$- to $\frac{3}{8}$- ounce) sometimes are used as well.

"Action" is the term used to describe the flexibility or stiffness a rod exhibits. Three actions are available:

Fast Action: This style bends very little; in fact, only the tip section will actually bend. A rod of this type is ideal when targeting large gamefish but isn't suited for crappie fishing.

Medium Action: A medium-action rod is the most common choice when the angler will be using various applications for a variety of species. These rods bend for about half their length, allowing an angler to fish both for small and large species with good control and hooksetting allowances.

Slow Action: A slow-action rod bends throughout nearly its whole length, providing the most flexible action available. These rods are used almost exclusively for panfish such as crappie, allowing a better fight for the angler. They also pro-

Rod Tips

- Sensitive rods help you detect more light-biting crappie. One way to determine if you have a rod that is truly sensitive is to rub the rod tip lightly across some corduroy cloth. If your rod is sensitive, you'll feel the material's texture.
- Check the guides on each rod before every fishing trip. If any are bent, straighten them or line will not flow through them correctly. Also, take a cotton swab and turn it inside each guide. If any cotton sticks to the inner portion of the guide, replace the guide before you use the rod again. If you do not, the line will fray or become nicked and could break when you set the hook on a crappie.
- When using a two-piece rod, rub a very light coating of paraffin onto the ferrule. This not only makes for a firm, secure connection, but also makes it easier to separate the sections.
- At home, it's best to store rods in a horizontal or vertical rack. Don't lean them against a wall or stack in a corner. If you do, each rod could become permanently bowed.
- Dirty cork rod handles can often be cleaned by sanding them with a very light grade of sandpaper.
- When motoring from one spot to another on a river or lake, always lay your rods flat. If you lean a rod against a sharp edge, the bouncing of the boat may score the blank, causing it to break when a fish is on.

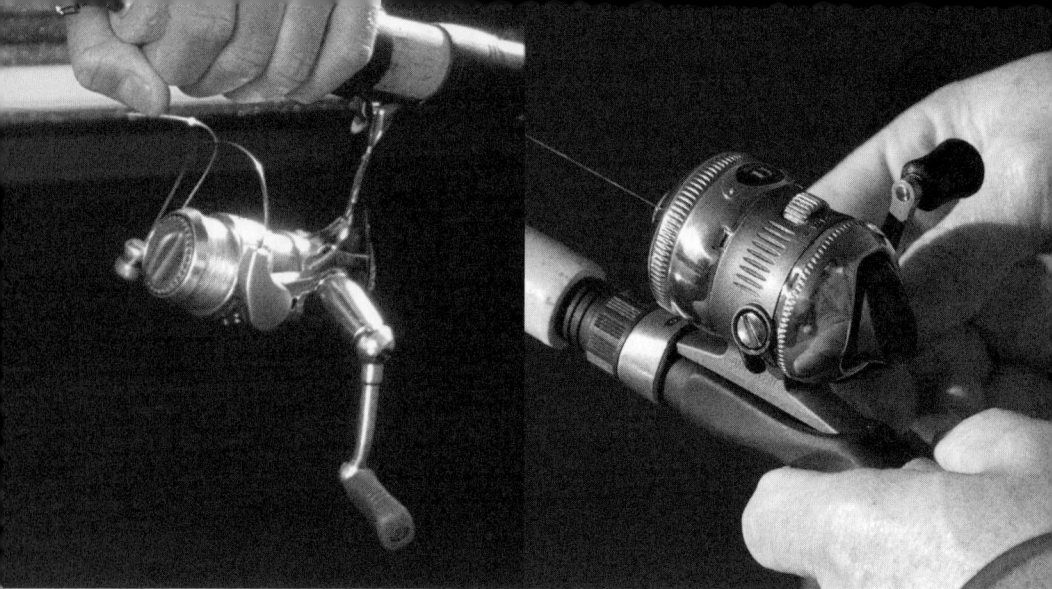

Spinning reels (left) work best with smaller-diameter lines but many crappie anglers still favor a spincast reel (right), which offers simpler casting and control.

vide "shock absorber" action so the hook is not ripped through the mouth when set, an important characteristic when fishing for "papermouths."

Before purchasing, you also should consider the rod's composition (fiberglass, graphite or graphite composite) just as you would the composition of a pole (see characteristics under "Poles").

When selecting a rod, keep these facts in mind as well. Spinning rods allow greater casting distance when using light lures. They have a different action than spincast rods. They also are better for landing fish on light line because there is significantly less friction caused by the guides. Spinning rod guides are on the underside of the blank. For these reasons, spinning tackle usually is the best choice if the angler using the outfit has no trouble casting with this type of combo.

Reels

Reels are available in three basic types: baitcasting, spinning and spincast.

Nearly all baitcasting reels are unsuitable for fishing the light lines, small lures and tiny baits used when crappie fishing. So most crappie anglers use either spinning or spincast reels.

Spinning reels, sometimes called open-face reels, are an ideal choice because they handle smaller-diameter lines well. However, spincast reels (also called push-button reels) are still the traditional favorites of many crappie fans. Spincast reels offer simple push-button casting control with a soft delivery suitable for minnows and other natural baits. And because they're simpler to use and rarely backlash or tangle, they're perfect for children and novice adults learning to cast.

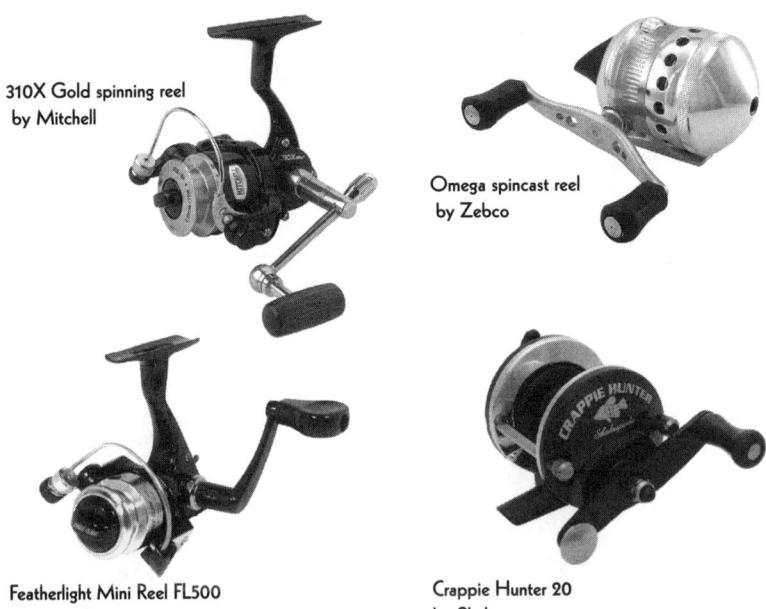

310X Gold spinning reel by Mitchell

Omega spincast reel by Zebco

Featherlight Mini Reel FL500 by Eagle Claw

Crappie Hunter 20 by Shakespeare

Reel Tips

- If you can't cast as far as you need to, switch to a spinning reel with a "long cast" style spool that is longer and shallower. On most reels, line flows freely when you first cast, but as the line level drops on the spool, the line must climb a steeper grade over the spool lip. This increased friction reduces the distance you can cast. With a long-cast spool, the shallower design keeps the lip smaller, thus casting distances are improved.
- If you purchased a new fishing reel and found it a little stiff when casting, take it apart and remove some of the gear grease. Old reels work better, too, if you clean out gummed-up grease and replace it with fresh. Most reels come with a tube of grease; use it.
- When setting your reel's drag, always do so by pulling line off the end of the rod, not directly off the reel's spool. That will give you the proper tension.
- When dismantling a reel for cleaning, place each part in a separate compartment of an empty egg carton as you go along. When reassembling the reel, pick up the parts in reverse order.
- Proper reel maintenance includes regular lubrication of all moving parts such as bearings, spool spindles and gears. Lubricate lightly, however, and do not use heavy oil, oil with a lot of wax or other additives or grease. These can gum up or leaves a residue that can inhibit movement of the bearings and other close-tolerance parts. Fine, light lubricants such as Rem Oil and X1R reel lube are excellent choices.

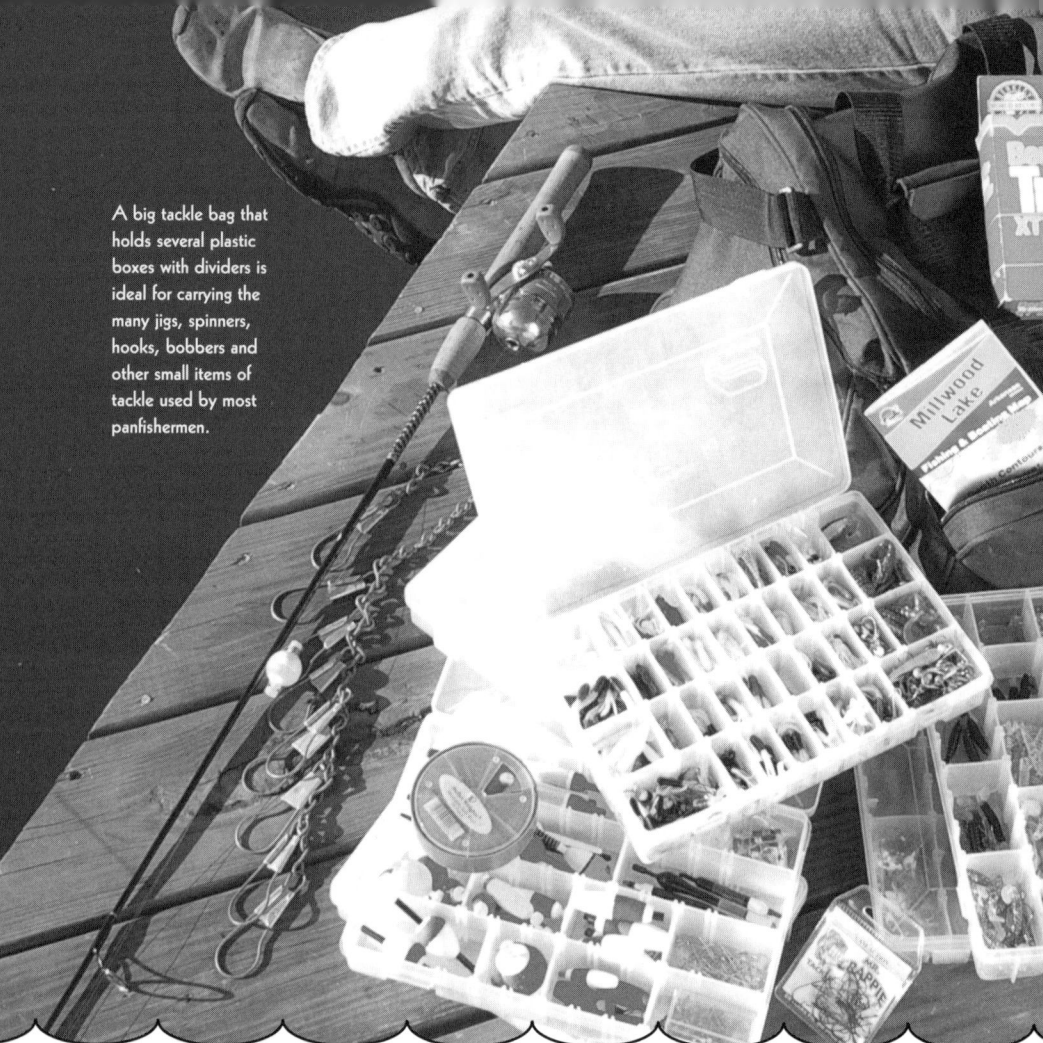

A big tackle bag that holds several plastic boxes with dividers is ideal for carrying the many jigs, spinners, hooks, bobbers and other small items of tackle used by most panfishermen.

How to Stuff a Crappie Tackle Box

My uncle, Guy McClintock, spent much of his life fishing for crappie. His fishing vessel was a 10-foot johnboat hand-crafted from cypress. His poles were hand-cut canes.

Not surprisingly, the tackle box he used was equally domestic—a coffee can into which he stuffed a few gold Aberdeen hooks, several yards of dacron fishing line, some small corks and an aspirin bottle filled with split shot.

A crappie fan who fishes like my uncle did—with minnows and cane poles—may need nothing more than a simple little tackle box to store terminal tackle and line. A coffee can will suffice, though you may want to shoot for something even simpler like a shoe box or Ziploc bag.

If you're like me, though, minnows and cane poles aren't enough to satisfy. I frequently fish with shiners, but I also like the satisfaction obtained from working jigs, spoons, crankbaits, spinners and other crappie lures. I love to fish with cane poles, especially when I'm trolling. But there are times when I'd rather be casting with a spinning combo or working heavy brush with a jigging pole. If the crappie are hard to entice, I may switch lures and poles several times, trying to find the perfect combination. Consequently, I prefer a large tackle box in which to carry all my fishing paraphernalia.

Here's some advice for selecting and stuffing a tackle box ideal for crappie fishing.

The Tackle Box

There are innumerable styles of tackle boxes on today's market. The one you select will depend largely on how much tackle you carry on each outing, the type of tackle you use and, if you're budget-conscious, the price.

If you're primarily a minnow fisherman, a small box to accommodate a selection of hooks, bobbers, sinkers and line may suit your needs perfectly. But if you fish both jigs and minnows, you'll probably want something more elaborate.

I tried a variety of tackle boxes—cloth bags, over-and-unders, tilt-trays and more—before finding my favorite. Most didn't have enough tray compartments to organize my jigs. And those that had an ample number of compartments didn't have space for larger tackle such as line spools and extra reels.

In the end, I settled on a large cloth tackle bag that holds several worm-proof, plastic boxes, each with dividers that can be custom-fit to create up to 24 compartments. I've configured the dividers so I have more than 100 compartments in which to organize different colors and sizes of jigs and jig heads, plus all the other lures and tackle I carry. The tackle bag also has several large pockets where I can store bulkier gear like stringers, line and reels.

Check out the variety of tackle boxes and bags available through your sporting goods dealer, study them to determine what type best suits your needs, then invest in a top-quality model and fill it with tackle to create your own ultimate crappie box. Here are some things you'll need to get started.

Terminal Tackle

In my tackle bag, I keep a small compartmented box for organizing hooks, sinkers and bobbers.

I prefer No. 1, 1/0 and 2/0 gold Aberdeen hooks. I keep several dozen of each size, mostly thin-wire models that do the least damage to fragile minnows and will bend enough to free from snags when fishing heavy brush.

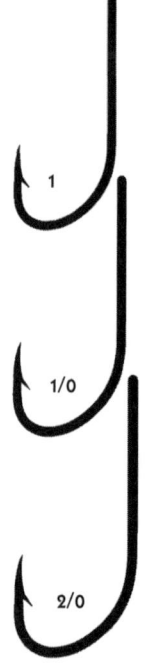

Crappie anglers who fish primarily with minnows may need only a small tackle carrier containing a few bobbers, sinkers and hooks.

Aberdeen Hooks

Split shot are the primary type of sinkers I use. I prefer those with small "ears" for easier removal, and generally have 100 or more in sizes 8 to 3 in my bag. Bobbers or floats are also important items of crappie equipment. In addition to suspending the bait at the right depth and providing a visual cue that a fish has taken the bait, they also add weight so you can better cast those tiny $1/64$- to $1/32$-ounce lures. I usually keep 15 to 20 in my tackle bag, including fixed bobbers and sliding bobbers made with foam, balsa and cork.

I keep an extra spool of 4- to 8-pound test line for situations dictating light line and a spool of 17 pound line I use when fishing heavy brush. I use premium monofilament and consider fluorescent green or yellow line best. These colors are more visible, which permits detection of the lightest strikes.

PALOMAR KNOT
Using this general-purpose knot makes tying on a hook as easy as 1, 2, 3.

1. Bend the line back on itself to form a double strand 6 inches long. Pass this double strand through the hook eye, and tie a loose overhand knot, leaving a loop deep enough so the hook (or lure) can pass through it.

2. Pass the hook through the loop, then tighten the knot by pulling the hook with one hand and the double strand of line with the other.

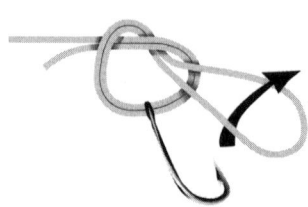

3. Trim the tag end.

Jigs and Other Lures

Jigs are my favorite crappie lures. To be prepared for any situation, my tackle bag contains several styles, colors and weights. Ninety percent are $1/32$-ounce, because that's the size I find most productive in most situations. However, there are times and places where smaller or larger jigs prove more productive, so I carry a variety of larger and smaller models as well.

It's a good idea to keep a variety of jigs in different colors, sizes and styles.

TRILENE KNOT
A multipurpose knot that can be used widely for tying on most hooks and lures.

1. Run approximately 4 inches of line through the hook eye, loop it around and pass it through the hook eye again. Pull the line to draw the loop down to a small diameter (¼-½ inch).

3. Pass the end back through the loop, and snug the knot tight by pulling the standing line and the hook in opposite directions.

2. Wrap the end of the line around the standing line 5 times.

4. Trim the tag end.

Chapter II: Tackle Tips

I also keep a variety of small, silver-bladed, safety-pin spinners in my tackle bag. These can be snapped on a jig to add extra crappie-attracting flashiness and vibration in stained or muddy water. In addition, I carry a small selection of other crappie-catching lures to use when jig fishing isn't productive. Among my favorites are ⅛- to ¼-ounce spoons, mini-crankbaits, small in-line and horsehead spinners, bladebaits and tailspinners.

Miscellaneous Equipment

The remaining equipment in my crappie bag consists of these items: an extra line-holder reel that will fit any of my jigging poles, an extra ultralight spinning reel, two stringers, a Gerber multi-tool, reel oil, sunscreen, nail clippers (for trimming line), a digital fish scale, a fish-scaler tool, a fillet knife and a ceramic knife sharpener. That's it. I have everything I need for most outings, and it's all together in a small package ready for transport.

Of course, there's no limit to the number of interesting items you can find to enhance your crappie fishing. And if you're like me, you'll be continually adding to your collection of "must-have" paraphernalia.

A few examples of the many useful "miscellaneous" items you may want to carry along.

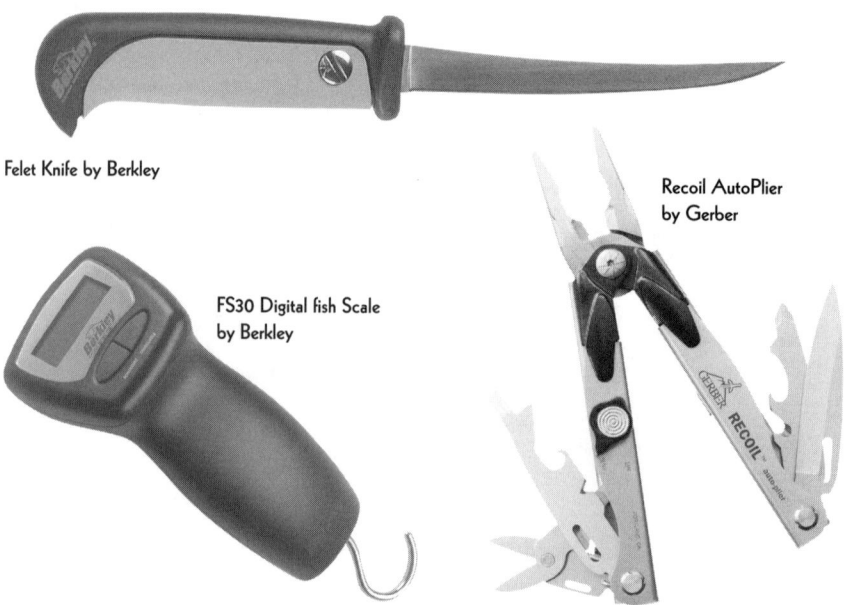

Felet Knife by Berkley

FS30 Digital fish Scale by Berkley

Recoil AutoPlier by Gerber

Tips for a Well-Stocked Tackle Box

Optional Items of Tackle
Here are some of additional items you may want to add to your crappie tackle:
- Bottom contour maps of fishing lakes
- Lighted floats for night fishing
- An electric fillet knife that runs off a 12-volt battery
- A pocket-size rainsuit
- Hook hone
- Fishing towel
- Emergency rod tip repair kit
- Battery-operated reel stripper
- Small marker buoys
- Compact binoculars
- Small, waterproof disposable camera
- Portable GPS unit
- Sheer pins and other spare parts for your outboard motor
- Small flashlight, signal flares and waterproof matches

Tackle Box Tip
- Save those little packets of silica gel that come packaged with so many electronic products. A few placed in your tackle box will absorb moisture and help prevent mildew.

Line Tips
- Fishing line can be ruined by direct sunlight or heat inside a vehicle. Keep reels and spools of line in cool, dark places when you're not on the water.
- When checking line for abrasions, don't feel with your fingers. Use your lips instead. Your lips are more sensitive than your fingertips, so you'll notice even tiny abrasions that can cause your line to break when you least it expect it. Retie your line at least once an hour, whether you feel nicks or not.
- Sometimes it's necessary to put new line on a reel while you're on the water. When this is done, many anglers keep the new line tight by running it through their hand or a wrapped towel. It's ok to do this, but be careful not to hold the line too tight. Heat generated by friction on the moving line can weaken the line. To be sure the line stays cool, you should wet your hand or the towel before you begin.

Bobber Tip
- One way to nab light-biting crappie is using a European-style "antenna" slip-bobber on 2- to 4-pound-test line. Run your line through the bobber, then add a bobber-stop above the float at the depth you want to fish. Tie on a jig, or a hook if you're fishing minnows, then start adding small split-shot between hook and float. Use enough weight so only ¼ inch of the bobber protrudes above the water. If a crappie swims upward after grabbing the bait, it removes some weight off the line, and the super-sensitive bobber rises enough to clearly indicate a taker.

Hook Tips
- Most crappie anglers prefer hooks made with wire that is relatively thin. If the wire has too great a diameter, your bait may die or swim unnaturally, and the hook won't bend enough to pull free when snagged.
- Sharp hooks catch more crappie. Check hook sharpness by dragging the hook across one of your fingernails. A hook that sticks or scratches the nail is sharp; one that doesn't isn't and should be honed.
- Safety pins can be used to hold and separate hooks of various sizes.

Chapter III

LURE SELECTION

Pick the Perfect Jig

This presents a dilemma for crappie anglers. How do you select the jig that will catch the most crappie? Are there certain conditions when one lure is preferable over another? When are big jigs more appropriate? Small ones? Is a jig with a spinner better or one without? Should a weedless jig be used or not?

There are no pat answers to these questions. I've seen days when crappie would hit everything from a $\frac{1}{100}$-ounce squirrel hair jig to a 1 ounce bass model. I've also seen days when crappie were so finicky they'd refuse all but a single offering. A black/red/yellow, soft-plastic tube jig might work, but a black/red/yellow marabou jig would not.

So, what's an angler to do? Start by applying the following

Jigs are the most popular and effective of all crappie lures, so it's important to know how to select the right jig from the many varieties available.

general guidelines when choosing jigs. You'll find these rules of thumb productive more often than not. On those occasions when they fail, don't fret. Yes, crappie can be persnickety. But if they're in actively feeding and you try enough variations, sooner or later you'll arrive at the perfect combination.

Matching the Hatch, So to Speak

One key to catching crappie consistently is using lures matching the size of the natural forage which the fish are accustomed to eating. Present a 1-inch jig to a school of crappie feeding on 2-inch baitfish, and there's a good chance you won't hook up. In fact, many expert anglers contend that imitating the size and shape of natural forage is more important to success than picking the right lure color.

How do you decide which size and shape is best? Because the predominant forage fish vary considerably from one body of water to another, from season to season, and even from day to day, the best way is to look at the stomach contents of crappie you catch. When you land a slab, see what's inside. If the fish is stuffed with tiny shiners, lures of that same general size and shape most likely will produce. The same holds true with other forage, such as shad or fathead minnows.

There will be times, of course, when you can't use this method because the crappie simply won't cooperate. In that case, try applying these general seasonal guidelines.

It's always smart to match jigs to the size of the predominant forage in the body of water you're fishing. For example, if 2-inch minnows comprise a large part of the crappie diet, use jigs that are the same size.

Spring

Crappie begin spawning activity when the water temperature is around 56 degrees. This occurs before most baitfish spawn. Consequently, most forage fish available for spawning crappie to eat are quite large. Some crappie will eat largemouth bass fry, which have just become available, but for the most part, food animals are larger than they will be during other seasons. For this reason, when fishing for bedding crappie, it is wise to mimic the predominant natural forage and use larger jigs. Versions up to ¼ ounce and three inches long produce well this season if slab crappie are your targets.

Big jigs produce in spring for another reason as well. Nesting crappie won't tolerate minnows or other small fish near their beds. So you'll often hit paydirt when you present a soft-plastic jig that has a big minnow- or shad-imitation body. The crappie will make a defensive strike to rid the nest site of the intruder, and you can savor the battle.

The colors, styles and sizes of jigs available to today's crappie angler seem almost endless.

Baitfish forming the bulk of the crappie's diet—gizzard and threadfin shad, for example, and several species of minnows—don't spawn until after crappie have spawned, when the water warms to 70 degrees. Spawning may continue at intervals throughout warm months, usually ceasing if the water temperature rises above 80 degrees or falls below 70 degrees. The bulk of spawning activity, however, occurs from mid-April through early June in mid-latitudes, and a bit earlier or later to the south and north.

When baitfish hatch, crappie suddenly have many sizes of forage animals on which to feed, from tiny fry to jumbo adults. After just a few days, however, the number of small baitfish far exceeds the number of adults. Crappie gorge on this bounty of fresh fry, stuffing themselves after a winter on lean rations.

Because crappie are eating mostly small forage fish, you'll probably catch more crappie by changing over to smaller jigs. When the water temperature is still near 70 degrees, most baitfish fry will still be tiny, and tiny jigs—$\frac{1}{100}$- to $\frac{1}{64}$-ounce, 1 inch or less—probably will be most enticing. By the time the water temperature rises above 75 degrees, many juvenile baitfish will exceed 1-inch long, and you may want to upsize your jigs to match this growth. A $\frac{1}{32}$-ounce or $\frac{1}{16}$-ounce jig, 1- to 1½- inches long, may now work as well as something smaller.

Summer

As spring turns to summer, baitfish near adult size. A threadfin shad, for example, may be two inches long at the first growing season's end. A gizzard shad may reach five inches. This means crappie have many larger baitfish on which to feed. In fact, from now through early autumn, large baitfish will be at peak abundance.

This is not to say, however, that big jigs are best this season. They certainly may work, but during summer, baitfish continue spawning periodically, and fry remain an abundant food source. Thus, crappie are regularly eating large baitfish and small. If the waters you fish don't get too hot too early, and if there's a good mix of large and small crappie, this is the one time of year when you can use any size jig and still expect consistent action.

It's important to remember, however, that much depends on the size of crappie available. For example, many waters are crowded with small crappie. In these, you may need to stick with smaller jigs—nothing over 1/32- or 1/16-ounce or 1 inch long—regardless of the season because an 8-ounce crappie is less likely to inhale a 1/8-ounce jig than a 2-pound crappie. Where crappie reach larger sizes, however, with a good mix of slabs and "barely keepers," stick with the seasonal guidelines presented here.

Autumn and Winter

In early autumn, expect summer patterns to continue. Crappie still find baitfish in many sizes and may strike a jig regardless of its size. As the water temperature falls, however, baitfish spawning activities cease, and the number of small baitfish drops as these fish grow or succumb to predation and cold weather. By the time winter is in full swing, the baitfish still alive tend to be larger on average than baitfish at other times.

This being the case, one would suspect that jigs with a larger silhouette would entice more winter crappie. I've found this to be true in the waters I fish, but only when the jigs are configured to allow a very slow presentation. The crappie's metabolism plunges when the water temperature falls, and the fish refuse to chase lures, even for short distances. Thus, jigs used to entice them must be presented very slowly. The lure should enter the fish's strike zone and remain there for best results.

This explains why many anglers downsize jigs in winter, even though most forage fish are large. The most elementary way to slow a lure's descent is to reduce the lure's size. Microjigs of 1/64 ounce and smaller drop through the water column at the agonizingly slow rate winter crappie prefer. Heavier jigs fall faster, often descending too quickly for lethargic crappie to strike. It would seem to make sense then that smaller lures would work better.

That might be true if downsizing your jig was the only way to slow it. But it's not. Another simple method is to use heavier line. Heavier line causes more resistance in the water, causing jigs to fall more slowly. In clear water, where line-shy fish are a concern, an easy solution is adding a foot or two of lighter leader between the main line and the jig. Another effective approach for reducing the fall rate is using a larger jig body (one bigger than what normally would be matched with a given jighead size) to create increased water resistance.

A bobber presents yet another means for fishing a jig slowly. A float rig allows the jig to be suspended, which means it can be worked at almost any pace, including a dead stop. If crappie are holding deeper than six feet, as they tend to do in winter, casting with a traditional float might be impractical. But a sliding bobber serves the same basic function and can be rigged with a bobber stop so it suspends your jig at the correct depth.

Knowing these things, we now can do a better job matching our jig to the size of most baitfish being eaten by cold-water crappie. If a stomach analysis finds crappie stuffed with two-inch shad, we can present a 2-inch, wide-bodied jig beneath a float, and work it very slowly at the depth crappie are suspended. When crappie forage consists primarily of large minnows, we can slow the presentation of properly matched jigs by using 15- or even 20-pound test line, with an added leader if necessary, or by using a 1/32-ounce jighead on a jig body more often used with a 1/16-ounce jighead. And so on.

In winter, when crappie bite slow-moving lures best, you can slow your jig presentation by downsizing the leadhead you use with a particular body style.

Other Considerations

It would be nice if the guidelines given above would work every time we go crappie fishing. Unfortunately, they won't. Successful crappie anglers consider many other facts as well.

For example, water clarity in the lake or reservoir we're fishing will considerably influence the right jig choice. In muddy water, crappie rely more on sound, vibrations and odor to find food. Thus, adding a spinner or rattling jighead to each jig may improve success. Clear-water crappie, on the other hand,

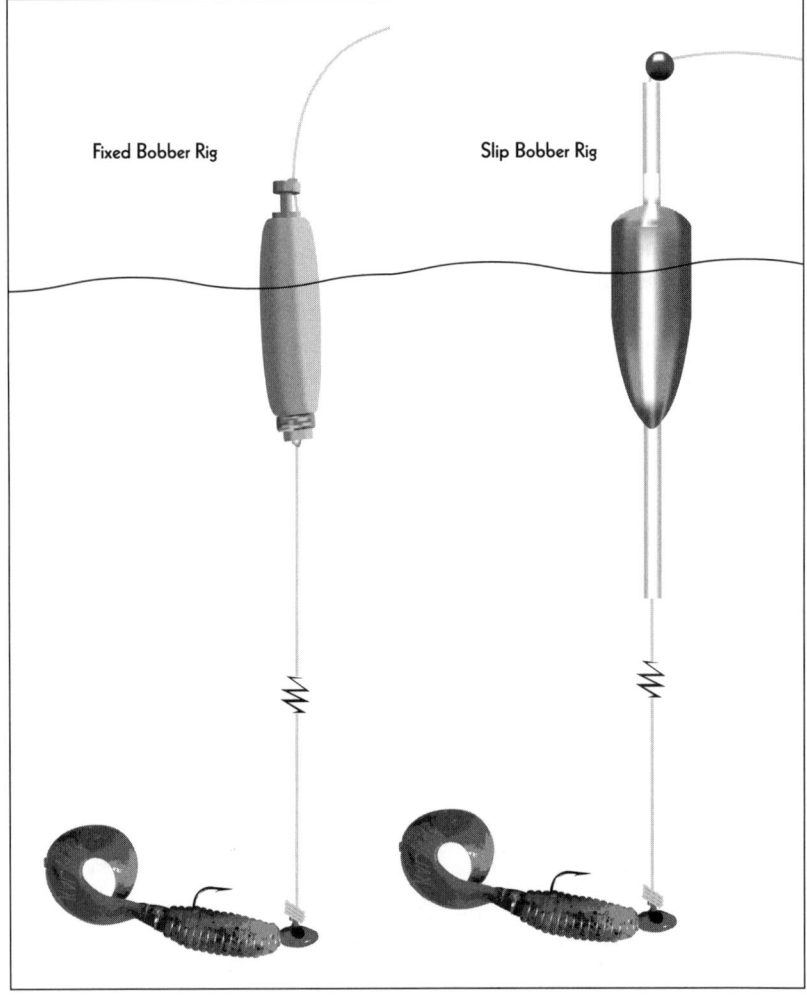

can better detect phony offerings, so it may be best to stick with smaller jigs they can't see as well. Jigs weighing $\frac{1}{32}$-ounce usually outproduce $\frac{1}{16}$-ounce jigs in this situation. Likewise, a $\frac{1}{64}$-ounce jig may be better than a $\frac{1}{32}$-ounce jig.

Are crappie hidden away in dense cover? If so, you may need to switch over to a weedless jig like Charlie Brewer's Crappie Slider. Are they feeding heavily on some type of insect or crustacean that's suddenly become abundant? Perhaps you should think about using a jig that more closely mimics one of these forage animals.

Sometimes crappie gather in dam tailwaters or other areas with heavy current. If so, you may need a heavier jig for proper presentation. A heavier jig may also help you reach deep summer crappie quicker.

When the fish get especially persnickety, you may need added enticements such as a curly tail or a jig where the soft-plastic body covers the entire leadhead. Scented jig bodies may be a bonus, or luminescent ones when fishing at night.

The variables you may encounter are nearly endless. But that's why the variety of jigs is nearly endless as well. If you carry a tackle box with a wide variety of styles and colors, and experiment with several variations, sooner or later you'll find the perfect combination.

"Do colors in jigs/lures/baits really make a difference? That's a constant question on the minds of crappie anglers nationwide. After more than 35 years of crappie fishing, I've found crappie seem to prefer brighter or fluorescent type skirts and leadheads on baits when there's dingy or muddy water. When fishing clear water, drop down to subdued colored skirts and unpainted leadheads. Dull colors such as clear with sparkle or motor oil are some good choices. However, be versatile and keep a buffet of colors in your jig box and let the fish decide which one they like best."

--Steve McCadams, www.stevemccadams.com

Jig Tips

- A jig/minnow combination sometimes works better than a jig alone. But when fishing this combo, especially in areas with current, the minnow has a tendency to separate from the jig hook. To prevent this, use a curly-tail jig Texas-rigged with a 1/8- or 1/4-ounce bullet weight on the line above the lure. Hook the minnow through the lips. Then turn the lure tail flat and impale the curly end on the hook. Pinch off the tail beyond the hook bend, and now, when the rig is worked across the rocky bottom, the minnow will stay hooked much longer.
- A tiny piece of minnow added to a jig hook maintains the jig's action while adding scent. Use a sharp knife to cut a fillet from the baitfish's side, then divide it lengthwise into two or more pieces. The added smell/taste increases your catch when finicky crappie avoid larger offerings.
- If you hook a crappie in the thin membrane around its mouth, the hook can tear out easily. To help eliminate this problem, bend the jig hook about 10 degrees outward from its original position. The hook is now more likely to stick in the roof of the crappie's mouth than in the membrane.
- Tired of losing jigs to snags? Carry along a 1-ounce bell sinker with a snap attached to the brass eye. When a jig gets hung, clip the sinker on your line and drop it. When the sinker hits the lure, it usually dislodges it. If not, jiggle your pole so the sinker bounces against the jig.
- Adding a scent product to your jigs may help you nab finicky slabs. Some products are sprayed on the outside of the lure. The best, however, are liquids or pastes you can "load" inside a tube. Do this by squeezing the tube lure, which is held with the open end up. As you inject the product into the tube, gradually release your hold on the tube. This pulls the scent inside, allowing it to be released more slowly than sprayed-on scent. Pellet-type scents can be shaped to the right size and pushed into the tube body for similar effect.
- If you pinpoint feeding crappie near schools of surface-running shad, try casting a 1/32-ounce jig tied above a 1/8-ounce jig with a small safety-pin spinner. The heavier jig stays well beneath the upper lure at a level where larger crappie are often holding. Double hookups are common.
- Many jigs now are available with glow-in-the-dark bodies and/or heads. Do they work? Sometimes yes, sometimes no, in my experience. But at times, when conventional jigs aren't producing, I've rigged with a luminescent version and started catching crappie after crappie. Rigging a small cyalume stick a foot or so ahead of the jig often improves effectiveness.

Safety-pin spinners are among the easiest to use of all crappie lures. Simply cast and retrieve, and get ready for action.

Spinners for Crappie

Spinners are almost irresistible to crappie because they exhibit vibration, flash and motion, all of which attract a fish's attention.

The vibration factor has great significance, especially in muddy water and after dark. Water is a positive conductor of sound waves, and crappie are very sensitive to vibrations and underwater noises. When water is murky or dark, sight feeding is hindered and crappie are more likely to strike a flashy lure that sends out lots of vibrations. Spinners do just that.

Spinners also allow fishing a greater area than can be done with jigs or minnows. This is especially significant when crappie are difficult to locate. The fisherman can tie on a spinner, cast to a likely looking spot, make a quick retrieve, and if a fish isn't caught, he can make another quick cast and retrieve in another spot. Jigs and minnows are more suited to a slow or stationary presentation and thus are less useful when trying to pinpoint crappie concentrations.

Also, because spinners are usually a little heavier than most other crappie lures, they can be cast longer distances with ultralight tackle. This allows you to stay farther away from the areas you're fishing. This often proves to be especially important quality when fishing clear waters where crappie are apt to be easily spooked.

Safety-Pin Spinners

My favorite type of spinner for crappie fishing is a safety-pin spinner clipped on a regular jig. The "spinner" part of this lure consists of a V-shaped wire frame. At the point of the V is a small line-tie loop. A small spinner blade is attached to the end of one arm with a swivel. At the end of the other arm is a small open-and-close clip to which you attach a jig or rubber grub. Perhaps the best known version of this lure is the Johnson Beetle-Spin.

Safety-pin spinners can cover a lot of territory when cast with ultralight gear, and they not only catch crappie, but an enormous variety of other sportfish as well. If you're not sure what type structure is beneath the water you're fishing, or if you're trying to figure out where crappie are located, take a little spinner like this and fan cast in a big circle to find fish. As you retrieve the lure, work it over, through and beside woody cover and other crappie hideouts.

Another nice thing about safety-pin spinners is the fact that it doesn't take a lot of expertise to use them. Fishing tiny jigs on a long pole requires a great deal of finesse and patience. Without these virtues, your lure will catch more snags than fish. Safety-pin spinners, on the other hand, are relatively weedless. A youngster or inexperienced angler with little casting experience can fish successfully with them.

The secret of fishing a safety-pin spinner is retrieving the lure as slowly as possible and running it close to the fish. When fishing shallow brush, blowdowns, weeds and other visible cover, cast beyond the cover and bring the lure through it or alongside it. It pays to live dangerously and bump the cover now and then with the lure, as this seems to excite crappie into biting. You'll get hung up some, but that's part of crappie fishing anyway.

If the jig or grub clipped to your spinner isn't producing, remove it and clip on a lure of different size or color. Some anglers even clip on flies like those used to catch trout, and under the right circumstances (during a spring mayfly hatch, for example), a spinner-and-fly combination can be an extremely effective crappie-catcher.

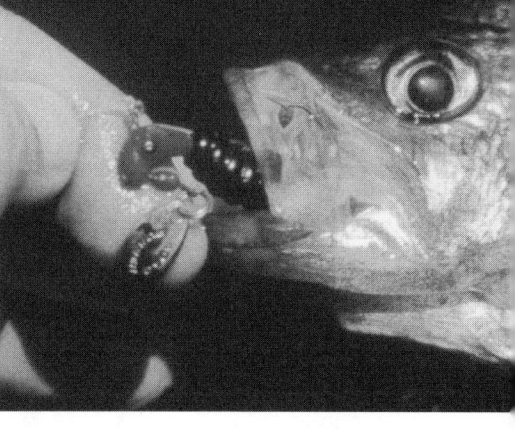

The tiny blade attached to the head of the horsehead spinner produces crappie-attracting flash and vibration.

Horsehead Spinners

Horsehead spinners such as the Blakemore Road Runner have been popular crappie lures for decades. These jewels are similar to regular leadhead jigs but have a uniquely shaped head with a tiny spinner attached it. Blakemore's marabou skirt model has sold in the millions, and their Turbo Tail with a soft plastic body is now a favorite, too. Both are dynamite crappie lures year-round.

Horsehead spinners are excellent for fishing points. Points are crappie hotspots year-round because they serve as a pathway for fish moving between shallow and deep water. By working a point methodically from shallow to deep water, you should be able to determine the day's depth pattern and use it to help locate crappie on other points or structural features.

Retrieve the spinner with an up and down "yo-yo" motion, or buzz it along the surface and allow it to fall or "die" beside fish-concentrating structure—stumps, fallen and standing timber, rocks, man-made brushpiles and the like. You can position your boat in deep water and cast toward the point's shallow end, or vice versa. If most crappie are caught around features at the point's upper end, then concentrate on shallow features when you move to other areas. If crappie seem to favor deeper areas on the point, you should continue fishing deep-water structure until you notice a shift in the pattern.

In-line (Weighted) Spinners

In-line, or weighted, spinners also are effective artificials for crappie. These are spinnerbaits constructed so the spinner blade revolves around a wire lure shaft rather than at the end of the shaft. Below the blade is a fairly heavy, metal body that can be almost any size, shape or color. Noteworthy examples include the Mepps Aglia, the Panther Martin Spinner, Wor-

In-line spinners come in hundreds of styles, colors and sizes, almost all of which catch crappie.

den's Rooster Tail and the Luhr-Jensen Shyster.

Because they're usually fitted with a small treble hook, in-line spinners are easily snagged when fishing brushy cover. To avoid this problem, concentrate on open-water structures—bridge pilings, riprap, rock outcroppings, boat docks, underwater points, submerged humps, etc.—where crappie are likely to be holding. In-lines also can be effectively fished along cover edges. Cast and retrieve along the borders of thickets, fish attractors, weed beds and other likely hideouts, avoiding tangles within the structure.

Some anglers like trolling with in-line spinners, but if the troll is too fast, the lures are inclined to spin and thus twist the line. A better tactic is to drift-fish with a light breeze that moves your boat slowly across the lake, or use an electric motor to maintain an ideal speed. Movement should be just fast enough to turn the lure's blade. Too fast and the lure "rides up" and twists your line. Too slow and the blade doesn't spin, rendering the lure ineffective. Done properly, this is an excellent technique for catching crappie suspended over inundated creek and river channels.

Spinners, like jigs and minnows, are part of the crappie buffet. And if you serve them up right, they can be every bit as effective as the old reliables.

Pro Tip

"When the water is stained, I like to take a Blakemore Road Runner and change the blade to a No. 3 gold willow-leaf blade. Big slabs can more easily find the customized lure in muddy to stained water."

--Kevin Rogers,
Crappie USA Classic qualifier six consecutive years

The Three Basic Types of Spinners

1. HORSEHEAD

Blackkore Road Runner

2. SAFTY-PIN

Johnson Beetle-Spin

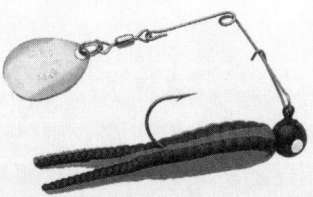

3. IN-LINE

Luhr Jensen Shyster

Spinner Tips

- Some crappie anglers like to "drop" spinners beside rock bluffs and creek channels. In this situation, a 1/16-ounce lure with a fairly large blade works best. The spinner is simply bounced down the drop-off on a tight line; rod tip movement controls the lure's fall. While the lure falls, the blade spins, and nearby crappie are likely to take the bait on the drop. Watch your line closely for slackening or sideways movement that indicates a hit.
- When crappie are finicky, remove the grub or tube body from a safety-pin spinner and replace it with a small live minnow. This small change may increase the number of fish you hook.
- Some of the best in-line spinners for crappie are those like the Mepps Comet Minnow that have a plastic minnow body in which the hooks are set.
- When a slower retrieve is desired, try using a sonic-type in-line spinner such as the Worden's Rooster Tail or Panther Martin. These have a blade that is concave on one end and convex on the other, so the blade turns very easily and will spin at a very slow retrieve speed.
- Check the clevis on your spinner (the U-shaped metal piece that holds the blade to the shaft) periodically to be sure it's not bent or fouled with bits of weeds. Straighten a bent clevis with needlenose pliers.

Relatively few anglers use crankbaits when fishing for crappie, but crankbaits resembling shad and other baitfish are superb enticements for these predatory panfish. Double hookups on single lures are always possible.

Crankbait Crappies

Today's savvy crappie anglers are innovative, often trying new tackle and tactics. Many have discovered that given the right set of circumstances, crankbaits are extremely effective crappie-catchers, despite the fact that few anglers use crankbaits when targeting these panfish.

Almost any small crankbait, and many large ones, can be used to entice crappie. I've used a 3½-inch Smithwick Rattling Rogue with great success in some waters, and Rebel's 1¼-inch Tadfry works great on shallow-water slabs. The best crankbaits, regardless of the size you use, are those that mimic the natural

Smithwick Rattling Rogue
Rebel Tadfry
Rebel Wee-R
Rebel Humpback

movements and colors of shad or other baitfish. And so you'll be prepared no matter where crappie happen to be, it's a good idea to carry a variety of crankbaits that can be worked at different depths. Carry some shallow-running models, some that suspend and others that are deep divers.

Crankbaits are especially productive during the spring spawning season. Crappie are very protective of their spawning grounds and will often hit these lures for that reason alone. Small floating/diving lures such as Rebel's Wee-R and ¼-ounce Humpback work especially well during this season. These lures float up away from snags when the retrieve is stopped, a necessity when fishing thick spawning cover.

If you want to move even further toward eliminating hang-ups, fish for crankbait crappie near bridge pilings, riprap, rock outcroppings, boat docks, weed edges and underwater points and humps where snags are less of a problem. In oxbow lakes, crappie often hold near the bases of big cypress trees where crankbaits also are very effective and hang-ups are less of a problem.

Deep-diving crankbaits are a real boon during summer, autumn and winter when crappie are in deep-water areas. During these seasons, use sonar to locate crappie-attracting structure. Then position your boat parallel to the structure, and work your lure slowly through the area.

Another time when crankbaits are very effective is in summer when crappie are schooling on the surface. During the dog days of

Work a crankbait just over the top of a weed bed to catch hungry summer crappie.

July and August, schools of crappie that normally hold in 15 to 25 feet of water will occasionally feed at the surface of lakes or rivers at dawn and dusk. Catching them is essentially like "jump" fishing for stripers or white bass running shad, but the surfacing crappie are not as noticeable.

To find top-running crappie, look for rough patches on otherwise smooth waters in large wooded coves. The crappie usually are chasing schools of small shad, and you can often see baitfish leaping from the water where fish are feeding. Many anglers think bass are responsible for the disturbances and spend gainless hours casting large plugs at them. But by quietly positioning your boat near the feeding school and tossing a shad-imitation crankbait into the melee, you can sometimes fill an ice chest with a mess of fat slabs.

Don't expect crappie to attack crankbaits with the ferocity of bass. Often, a crappie only nips at the lure rather than hitting it hard. When you feel a crappie tapping the lure, stop reeling, drop the rod tip, and take up slack. Then raise the rod on a tight line, and you usually will have the fish hooked. When the lure stops, the crappie probably thinks it has injured the prey and quickly pounces on it before one of its schoolmates grabs the easy meal.

Jigs and minnows will be the mainstays for crappie anglers as long as there are crappie to catch. Papermouth fans love to see the bobber go under, to feel the bow in their jigging pole. But when crappie are just a little bit finicky, when old-fashioned techniques just won't produce, try the crankbait option. You may be glad you did.

Lipless crankbaits are great crappie locators. The narrow body has little wind or water resistance, so you can cast long distances and retrieve rapidly, combing broad areas to find active biters.

Secret Weapon: Lipless Crankbaits

All types of crankbaits can be used to catch crappie, but lipless crankbaits deserve further discussion because of their extreme versatility. Anglers can use them at all depths, in muddy water and clear, during all seasons and in almost any cover. Without changing lures, you can jig in deep-water timber, count down to crappie suspended by bridge pilings or buzz across the top of a brushpile. Best of all is their simplicity; anyone can fish these lures.

Lipless crankbaits go by a variety of names, including slab plugs, vibrators, rattlers, rattlebaits and sonics. Many compa-

Bill Lewis Bleeding Shad Rat-L-Trap lipless crankbait.

nies manufacture them. At the head of the pack is Bill Lewis Lures of Alexandria, Louisiana, maker of the famous Rat-L-Trap. This wasn't the first such lure, but Lewis' Rat-L-Trap is so well-known, its name is synonymous with lipless crankbaits.

Lipless crankbaits come in floating and sinking models, and in sizes ranging from tiny ($\frac{1}{10}$ ounce) to large (over 1 ounce). Smaller models—1 to 2½ inches long, $\frac{1}{10}$ to ½ ounce—work best on crappie because they're similar in size to the baitfish crappie feed on. Don't reject the larger sizes automatically, however. I've caught many crappie on bass-sized models, even though these don't take crappie with the regularity of shorter, lighter-weight lipless crankbaits that are more easily inhaled.

Each lipless crankbait has a line-tie eye on the back, which makes the lure run with its head angled down. Water pressure on the typically flat forehead produces a tight, convulsive, shimmy that closely resembles a small baitfish zipping through the water. Crappie find this action irresistible.

Most models also contain sound-producing pellets. The lure's tight, fast vibration whips the pellets against the sides of the bait, creating a rattle that sometimes can be heard 50 feet from the boat. This clattering noise is especially important for enticing strikes in muddy water or dense cover, at night and on windy days.

Most anglers fish vibrators like other crankbaits, simply casting them out and reeling them back in, varying the retrieve speed and pausing occasionally. You also can fish them like bass jigs, casting the lure and letting it sink, giving it a good hard lift with the rod and reeling in the slack as it sinks again.

Vertical jigging is highly effective on summer and winter crappie suspended around deep ledges, weed lines, bridge pilings, sunken islands, bluffs and isolated brush piles. Position your boat directly over the target structure, then lower the lure until you feel it hit bottom. Engage your reel and take up slack. Then begin a delicate upward sweep of the rod tip to activate the vibrator. Move the rod tip as little as 12 inches or as much as 36 inches, experimenting as you fish to determine if crappie have a preference. Then slowly drop the rod tip, letting the lure free-fall. Maneuver your boat along or around the structure, jigging the lure this way. And set the hook the instant you feel a hit. Strikes nearly always occur as the lure is spiraling downward, but most strikes go undetected until pressure is applied to the lure on the upward sweep.

A similar tactic is effective for fishing shallow sunken timber. Use a long jigging pole or fly rod to lower the lure near the structure—similar to a jig presentation, but give the lure considerably more action. Flicks of the wrist load a long rod, making the lure hop erratically. Watch your line carefully for any slackening or jerk that indicates a strike.

During the prespawn period in early spring, crappie begin following creek channels and other sharp-edged bottom structure toward their spawning areas. Anglers searching for them must cover lots of water, and lipless crankbaits are great for this. Cast and retrieve them around staging areas such as secondary creek channels, outside creek bends and bottom channel junctures. Creek channels circling humps or small ridges also are key spots.

As water temperature climbs, crappie move nearer to their spawning sites. Cast for them on shallow flats close to deep water. When spawning activity is underway, most anglers stop using lipless crankbaits, putting them away until crappie leave the beds and move back to deeper water. But they remain effective throughout this season, especially where spawning beds are in more open water.

In late spring and early summer, try working your lures over the tops of submerged weedbeds. If the vegetation is just a foot or two under the surface, many anglers use a floating vibrator on 10-pound-test line. Retrieve with your rod tip low, alternately reeling to draw the lure under the surface, then pausing so it floats back up. When the plants are deeper, use a sinking model and count it down to the top of the vegeta-

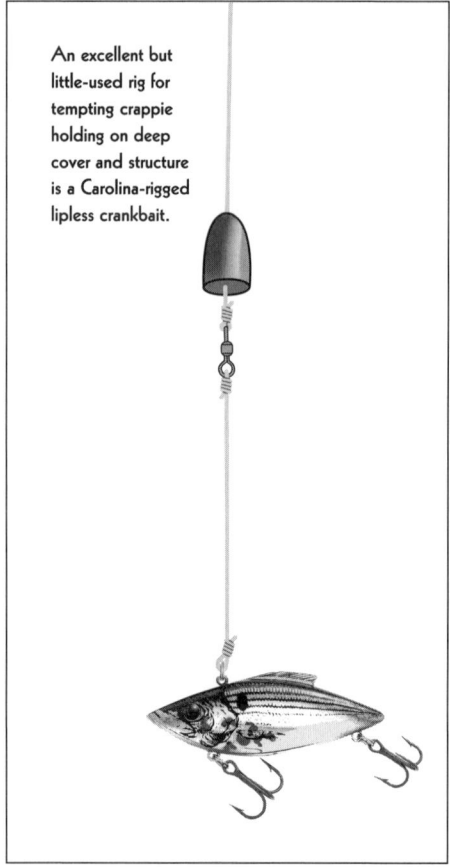

An excellent but little-used rig for tempting crappie holding on deep cover and structure is a Carolina-rigged lipless crankbait.

tion before starting it back. Ideally, the lure should just tick the top of the weedbed on your retrieve. If it moves too fast over the weeds without hitting any, it's not nearly as effective.

A sliding-bobber presentation also works in this situation. Simply tie a small vibrator beneath a sliding bobber that's adjusted to place the lure just above the weeds. Cast, let the lure settle, then jig, bringing the line through the bobber to make the lure vibrate.

A few innovative crappie anglers are now using lipless crankbaits on Carolina rigs, a very effective technique when crappie are holding deep near bottom structure. Use a floating lure, a half-ounce sinker and a leader of about 24 inches so you'll have good line control. With this rig, you can use almost any retrieve imaginable. The crankbait floats above the bottom, and each jerk makes the lure dive and swim erratically.

Versatility like this is what makes the tiny lipless crankbait one of the best of all crappie lures. Every crappie angler should learn the many ways to fish this extraordinary bait.

Crankbait Tips

- Crappie often hold around submerged beds of green aquatic vegetation such as coontail. Test these waters for slabs by drifting or fan-casting crankbaits over the weed beds. If the vegetation rises near the surface, use floating-minnow imitations and work them with jerky retrieves so they tickle the tops of the cover. When weed tops are separated from the surface by a few feet of water, try a suspending minnow crankbait. Where weed tops are deep, and in places where weeds are sparse, try a deeper-diving, shad-imitation crankbait worked between the stalks.
- To catch crappie suspended in open water near tributary mouths, watch for boomerangs on your sonar, then try trolling crankbaits instead of jigs. Use a $1/4$ to $1/8$ ounce diver. Silver works great on sunny days and in clear water. If the sky is overcast, or the water is murky, switch to hot colors such as chartreuse.
- Crappie often hold on points sloping toward bottom channels. Among the best lures for fishing these areas are small, deep-diving, baitfish-imitating crankbaits. It's difficult to keep crankbaits at favored depths and still move them slow enough to entice lethargic crappie. Using a neutral buoyancy or sinking crankbait eliminates these problems. Using light line—4 to 6 pound-test—crank the lure down to the proper depth then slowly crawl it across the bottom, retrieving the lure from shallow water to deep, or working across the point toward the deepest side. Crank your lure hard and fast several turns to get it near bottom before slowing to an effective pace. If possible, bump the lure against stumps, logs, boulders, etc. to elicit strikes.

Lipless Crankbait Tips

- For the best action, attach a lipless crankbait to your line with a loop knot or small O-ring, never with a snap swivel or heavy leader.
- The smallest lipless crankbaits work best with the lightest line needed for a particular fishing situation. In open water—around docks, bridge piers, outer edges of weed beds, etc.—2 to 4 pound test is usually sufficient. When fishing around dense woody cover, 8-pound-test works well, although with some of the tiniest lures, the vibration may be somewhat compromised.
- A sensitive rod helps detect changes in vibration that could signal a strike or indicate the plug has fouled. Rods also should be stiff enough to activate the lure with the least amount of rod movement. A light graphite, 6-foot spinning rod with a fairly stiff butt and flexible tip works well.
- Try to match the lure's size to the size of the predominant baitfish. In late winter and early spring, for instance, larger lures may work better because small, young-of-the-year baitfish are not yet available. Switch to smaller lures in summer after baitfish spawn.
- The size of a lipless crankbait is not usually an impediment to generating strikes from crappie, but the size of stock hooks may prevent successful hookups. On larger lipless crankbaits, replace larger hooks with size No. 6 to increase your catch.

Weedless spoons like the Johnson Silver Minnow work great when fishing deep weed beds and similar cover.

Pumping Iron: Catching Crappie on Spoons

Like crankbaits, spoons hardly rate a second glance with most crappie anglers, even though they're extremely effective under certain conditions. A properly worked spoon closely resembles a dead or dying baitfish fluttering through the water, and crappie find it hard to resist. Spoons are used in a variety of fishing situations, but they're especially productive for catching prespawn and postspawn crappies suspended in deep water.

Spoons are classified in two primary groups: 1) casting and trolling spoons, which have a curved body, and 2) jigging spoons, which generally have a flatter, thicker body. When fishing open waters where hang-ups aren't much of a problem, casting and trolling spoons can be used. Open-water fishing isn't the norm when crappie are targeted, however, so casting and trolling spoons have limited applications. Jigging spoons, on the other hand, are blue-ribbon enticements to use when fishing standing timber and other crappie cover that can be worked using a vertical technique.

Replacing the treble of a spoon with a single hook may help increase hook-sets and allows fish to be released unharmed if desired.

Stick to smaller spoons—$1/32$- to $1/6$-ounce—because these are easier for crappie to get in their mouths. Position your boat over or beside the target structure, then lower the lure until it hits bottom or to a depth where your sonar shows crappie are suspended. Engage your reel and take up slack, sweep your rod tip upward one to three feet, then slowly drop the rod tip, letting the lure free-fall. Repeat this procedure for a while, and if a strike isn't forthcoming, change to a different depth.

Most strikes come as the spoon falls and feel like faint taps or a "heaviness" on the line. Braids and other low-stretch lines are especially good for this type of fishing because of their high sensitivity, which telegraphs each strike. A fast-action rod may work better than the medium- or slow-action rods typically used for crappie fishing because a too-limber rod decreases sensitivity and makes strike detection and hooksetting more difficult.

If you're fishing around woody cover, the spoon's treble hook is likely to snag now and then. But the spoon's weight will help unsnag it if you have a direct line of pull overhead.

When fishing shallow timber, try using a long jigging pole or fly rod to lower a spoon near the cover. Flicks of the wrist load a long rod, making the spoon hop erratically. Watch your line carefully for any slackening that indicates a strike.

A guide on Missouri's Truman Lake gave me a refresher course on spoon fishing that's worth relating. We motored to a band of dead trees lining a river channel. "These trees look alike," he said. "But there's a fence corner that comes up to these two. It was inundated when the dam was closed, but a couple of cedar trees still stand there, and they attract lots of nice crappie."

Chapter III: Lure Selection

I tied on a green-and-black jig as the guide instructed, but after 15 minutes, no crappie had fallen for it. The blue-and-white jig on the guide's line also was ineffective.

"Maybe the crappie aren't here today," I suggested.

"On the contrary," he said. "Ninety times out of a hundred, I'll catch a dozen or more crappie in this spot. They're here. We have to figure out what they want."

Minnows drew no strikes, nor small spinners. But when the guide lowered a jigging spoon into the cedars, he hooked a slab. Over the next hour, spoons produced 30 fat crappie for us.

"Don't give up on a previously productive fishing spot too quick," the guide told me. "Sometimes crappie are persnickety; they want something different. That's when small spoons often work."

Remember that next time you find crappie hard to catch.

Spoon Tips

- One way to nail barn-door crappie is working big weedless spoons in and around timber, brush and weed beds adjacent to fast-breaking bottom structure. Effective models include the ¼- or ½-ounce Johnson Silver Minnow, the ½-ounce Johnson Silver Minnow Spinner Spoon and the ½-ounce Cabela's Real Image Weedless Spoon.
- Hooks are easily changed on spoons. Some anglers like to remove the treble hook that comes on some models and replace it with a single hook that provides better hooksetting penetration and permits the release of more fish alive when desired.
- Spoons often twist line. To combat this, use a high-quality ball-bearing swivel above a leader to which the spoon is tied, and if necessary use a snap swivel to attach the spoon.
- Bending a jigging spoon will alter its action. A bent spoon flutters more erratically as it sinks.
- Many spoons come with poor-quality, dull nickel hooks. Replace these with sharper bronze hooks that straighten more easily when you get snagged.
- If you're jigging a spoon around suspended crappie you've seen on your depth sounder, be sure to reel the lure up and jig it just above the fish, not below them. Crappie often look up for food but rarely look down.

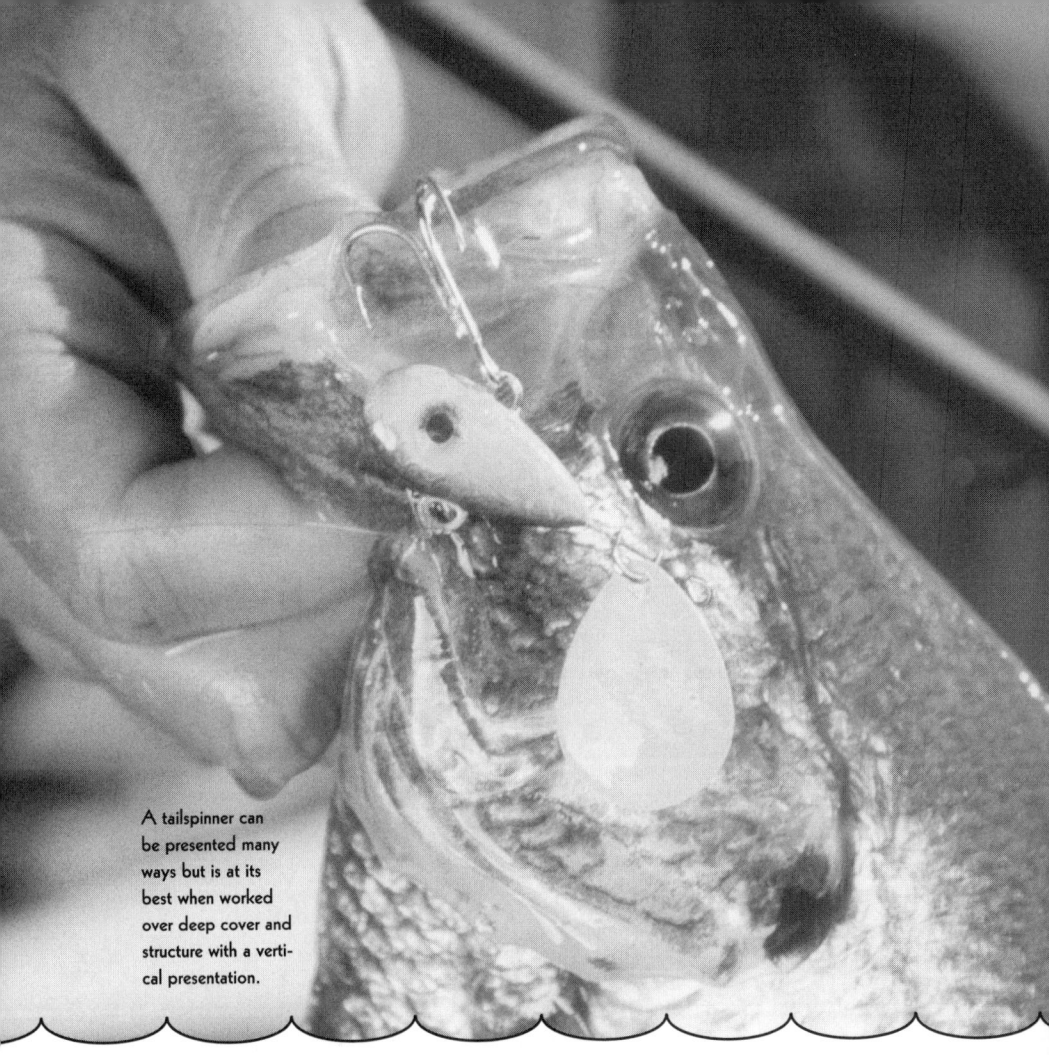

A tailspinner can be presented many ways but is at its best when worked over deep cover and structure with a vertical presentation.

Heavy Metal: Bladebaits & Tailspinners

Like jigging spoons, bladebaits and tailspinners are renegade lures often considered outcasts by crappie fishermen brought up on a strict diet of jigs and minnows. Nevertheless, both lure types are proven crappie-catchers, and each has unique characteristics that make it applicable to special situations.

Bladebaits

The Heddon Sonar was the first mass-marketed bladebait, circa 1959, followed a few years later by Cotton Cordell's Gay Blade. Both lures are constructed with a stamped metal blade shaped

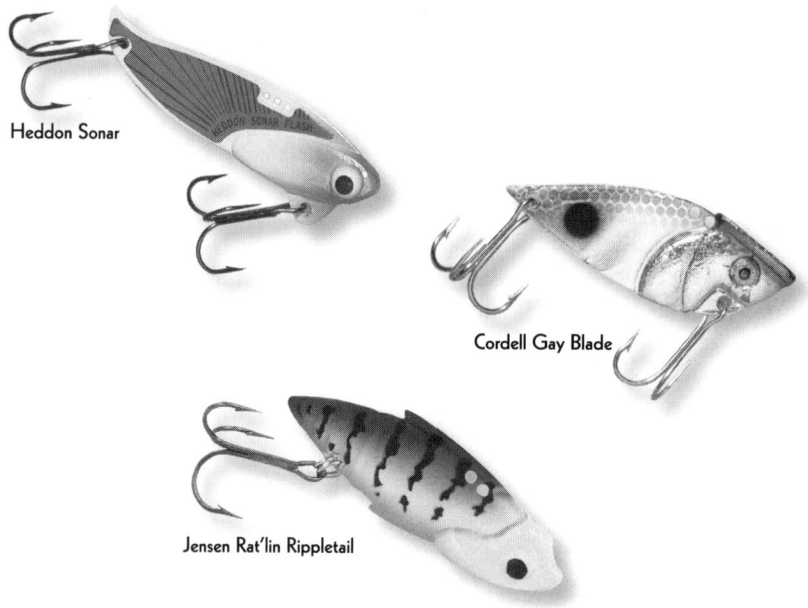

Heddon Sonar

Cordell Gay Blade

Jensen Rat'lin Rippletail

somewhat like a baitfish. This is sandwiched between pieces of lead that form the "head," with line-tie holes on the blade's top edge and holes for two treble hooks on the bottom.

Although this basic design is the starting point for all bladebaits, each manufacturer today (there are several) has created a bladebait unique in shape, size and weight distribution. For example, while the bodies on the Sonar and Gay Blade are both straight and sleek, the position and contour of their heavy heads produce different actions. Luhr Jensen's Rat'lin Rippletail and Reef Runner's Cicada have proportionally wider bodies with wavy and cupped tails. Such variations give each lure a unique action.

Bladebaits originally came in one color, silver, and one finish, flat. Manufactured blades now come in gold, copper and brass base colors. Finishes can be flat, hammered or rippled. Painted finishes have been added, too, giving anglers many color choices.

When water is cold and crappie are deep, bladebaits can be hot. Snapped upward, they swim through the water and create a pulsating vibration that mimics an injured or escaping baitfish. This attracts and allows a crappie to home in on the lure, especially when water is murky. You can vertically jig a bladebait to create a subtle swimming and fluttering motion, effective at attracting skittish, light-biting crappie; or retrieve it with occasional rips and runs to produce a dynamic, erratic action that might interest a slab in need of a wake-up call.

Bladebaits also are effective when targeting deep summer crappie on drop-offs and humps. When fishing dropoffs, keep your boat directly over the drop and cast to the top of the breakline, hopping the lure back to the boat. When fishing humps, position the boat off the hump and cast to the rise, working the bait on top first, then down the sides into deep water.

Most bladebait strikes occur on the fall. Watch your line closely and keep it tight during the retrieve.

Smaller bladebaits, ¼- to ½-ounce, generally work best for crappie, but bigger models can produce where 2-pound-plus crappie are expected.

Some bladebaits have two or three holes on the top edge for line connection. Each placement allows for a different vibrating action, so read the manufacturer's instructions detailing which hole is most suitable for various applications. If there are two holes, generally the front one, with its tighter wiggling action and less vibration, is the best bet for vertical jigging. When three holes are available, choose the center one.

Never tie your line directly to a bladebait. One good smack from a crappie and the thin metal body will shear monofilament like thread. Use a round-bend snap or a split-ring to make the connection.

A bladebait swimming through the water creates a pulsating vibration that imitates and injured baitfish. Slab crappie find these lures hard to resist.

Tailspinners

Tailspinners generally have a teardrop-shaped body made of lead or alloy. A spinner blade revolves on a wire shaft protruding from the tail. In 1960, fishing legend Tom Mann created the best-known version, the Little George, to meet his need for a versatile lure that could be burned across the surface or crawled along the bottom. Mann made the Little George primarily for bass fishing, but small versions proved to be superb crappie lures as well.

Two characteristics give tailspinners their deadly action. First, the line tie on top of the lure keeps the lure balanced, allowing the blades to spin or "helicopter" as the lure falls. This helicopter action triggers most strikes. Second, the spinner blade is attached directly to the lure body, which causes the body to vibrate. This fish-attracting shimmy makes tailspinners effective in any water-color situation.

Tailspinners can be fished several different ways. Whichever tactic is used, it is vital to keep a tight line during retrieve. Strikes are subtle. Often, the lure is inhaled as it helicopters down. Using a sensitive rod and keeping your line tight will help detect these soft strikes.

When fishing for deep summer and winter crappie, try casting the lure to structure or cover and allowing it to settle on the bottom. Then, with your rod tip high, retrieve the tailspinner just fast enough to keep it off the bottom.

Vertical presentations often are called for when sluggish winter crappie are holding tight to the bottom or suspended in submerged standing timber. Position your boat directly over the fish and lower a tailspinner to the level where fish are marked on your electronics. Slowly lift your rod a foot or two, then drop the rod with a tight line, controlling the rate at which the lure falls. The tailspinner should descend just fast enough to make the blade spin.

Mann's Little George

Bladebait Tips

- You can add noise to a bladebait's vibrations for even more crappie attraction. Visit a sewing craft shop and purchase stick-on eyes with little black plastic balls inside the eye dome, then add them to the head of each lure.
- Some anglers like to customize bladebaits by slightly adjusting the blades using pliers. Alter the blade so it is cupped or concave, and you'll create new action and vibration qualities, and change the descent speed.
- Use glitter nail polish to add a reflective color to bladebaits that looks like tiny scales.
- Most bladebaits have two treble hooks. A recent trend, however, is to replace these with two dual hooks. The hooks facing the center of the blade are removed. You can buy dual hooks or use wire cutters to snap off the third hook on each treble. Some anglers remove the forward treble altogether to reduce snagging.

Tailspinner Tips

- Tailspinners are great for targeting schooling summer crappie feeding on shad at the surface. Because tailspinners can be cast "a country mile," they allow anglers to keep their distance from the feeding crappie.
- Try a tailspinner as a follow-up lure when fishing deep-water ledges and points. When crappie quit biting other lures, cast a tailspinner to check for suspended or inactive fish. Cast the lure; when it hits bottom, rip it hard and let it flutter back down. This imitates dying shad, which are irresistible crappie enticements.
- You can also try a quick retrieve to bring the lure over the top of weed beds or cover. The vibration and flash often draw strikes.
- When trying to pinpoint crappie on vertical structure such as bridge pilings or slick standing timber, cast a tailspinner and swim it through the top of the water column. On successive casts, retrieve at different depths. Continue going deeper until you end up jigging it straight down. Crappie can be at any depth on such structure—5, 10, 20 feet or deeper. In summer, they're usually in the top 10 feet, but in winter they may be in 30 feet. With a tailspinner, it's possible to cover all the depths effectively by slowly working the bait down a level at a time.

Chapter IV

CONSIDERING BAIT

Crappie Fishing with Minnows

Minnows are an inseparable part of crappie fishing. Although adult crappie feed on other forage as well, small fish make up most of their diet. And because minnows can be raised commercially and are available at bait shops throughout the U.S., they're the bait of choice for many crappie anglers.

The word minnow is often used to describe any small, silvery fish. But technically, minnows are members of the family *Cyprinidae*, the largest fish family in North America. Some of the 200 species in the U.S., such as the grass carp and goldfish, grow quite large. But most native groups such as shiners, daces and chubs seldom exceed four inches.

The species most used by crappie anglers are the golden shiner

Live minnows are among the best of all enticements for crappie. They often catch fish when nothing else will.

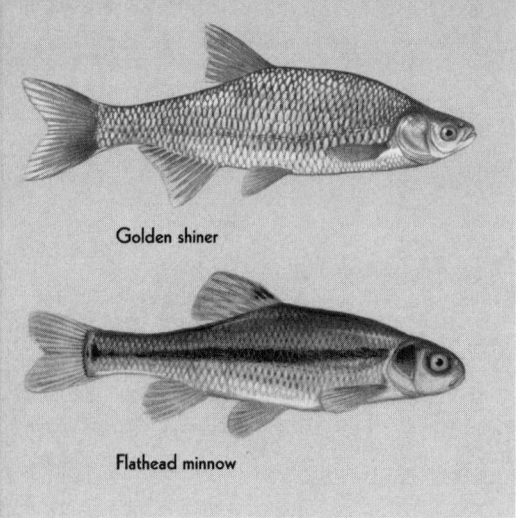

Golden shiner

Flathead minnow

and fathead minnow, both produced by the tons on commercial fish farms. Arkansas leads the country in production, with some six billion minnows raised annually (61 percent of U.S. total). Species preference in selected regions of the U.S. indicates golden shiners are most popular with anglers in the Southeast, Southwest and West, while fathead minnows are the dominant species in the Northeast and Midwest.

Farm-raised minnows aren't the only baits used by crappie fishermen. Many anglers catch wild baitfish with traps or nets. In fact, according to some estimates, about half of all baitfish are still caught from the wild. Species often used by crappie an-

Minnow Buckets

Minnow buckets usually are made from metal, plastic, styrofoam or a combination of these materials. Many anglers prefer metal or plastic buckets instead of styrofoam because they are more durable. However, several styrofoam buckets can be purchased for the price of a single metal or plastic bucket, and there's evidence that minnows may stay much livelier in a styrofoam bucket.

In his book, *Advanced Crappie Secrets*, crappie researcher Steve Wunderle tells about experimenting with styrofoam, plastic and metal minnow buckets to determine if minnows survived longer in one or another. He found styrofoam buckets superior for keeping minnows alive during late spring, summer and fall, largely because water in styrofoam buckets stays cooler longer. In fact, none of the 48 minnows in the styrofoam buckets Wunderle tested had died after eight hours, while half or more of the minnows perished in the other bucket types during the same time.

This is an extremely simplistic overview of Wunderle's experiment and results, which you should obtain and read. But it does point to the fact that styrofoam minnow buckets may be better at keeping minnows frisky than buckets of plastic or metal throughout most of the year.

Today, anglers can buy plastic buckets with styrofoam liners that provide both durability and temperature control. In hot weather, they're ideal for keeping minnows cool and lively. They work great for ice fishing, as well, because they have less of a tendency to split or crack than styrofoam alone. The bucket's hard outer shell protects the foam inner liner.

Also available are trolling-style buckets that have a more hydrodynamic shape to pull easily through the water behind a boat or a wading angler. Most are made to float face-up for easy access to the bait, and each has small slits or openings that allow water to flow through and aerate the minnows. If you troll a lot, these are worthy of consideration.

glers include the bluntnose minnow, blacknose dace, creek chub, hornyhead chub, common and red shiner, and mudminnow.

Many regulations govern the use, collection and sale of minnows. These often are aimed at protecting waters from introductions of exotic species that could wreak havoc on the ecosystem. In some areas, only live minnows are prohibited. In others, minnows of any sort—live or dead—may be banned. Capture of wild fish is closely regulated in many areas as well. And if you catch baitfish to sell or use, you may need a special permit. Considering these things, it's important to study all regulations carefully before using minnows as bait.

Keeping Minnows Lively

In fishing, subtleties often make the difference between a good day or bad day on the water. Nowhere is this truer than when using live bait such as minnows. Sickly or dead minnows might work ok if you locate a school of super-aggressive crappie. Typically, however, sluggish, barely alive minnows won't catch as many crappie as frisky, healthy baits. It's important, therefore, to keep your minnows lively, something many crappie anglers find difficult to do.

One important consideration is the hardiness of the minnows you use. Fathead minnows are hardier than golden shiners, for example, being better able to withstand drastic changes in water temperature, low oxygen levels and rough handling. Golden shiners, on the other hand, are hardier than emerald shiners.

It's also important to use healthy minnows. Healthy minnows

MINNOW HARDINESS GUIDE

Use this hardiness guide to select the best types of baitfish for your crappie fishing. The hardiest species are generally the liveliest on the hook.

- **Very Hardy:** fathead minnows, mudminnows, goldfish
- **Moderately Hardy:** young bluegills, creek chubs, hornyhead chubs, southern redbelly dace, blacknose dace, bluntnose minnows
- **Somewhat Hardy:** golden shiners, common shiners, red shiners, banded killifish
- **Least Hardy:** emerald shiners, small gizzard or threadfin shad, spottail shiners

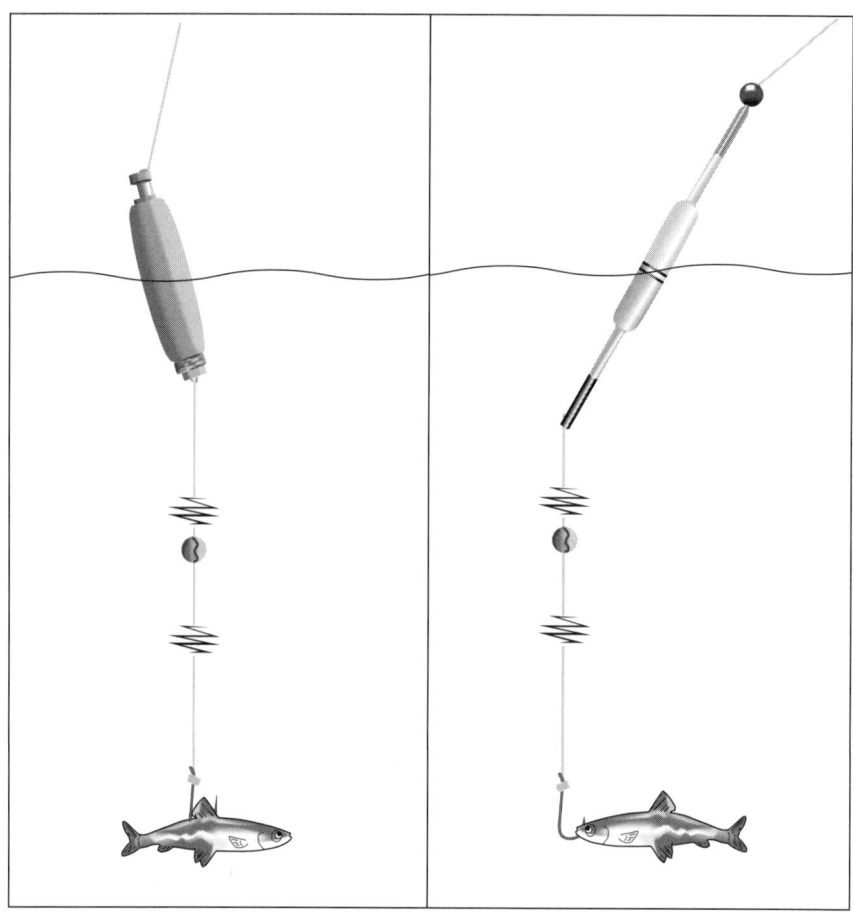

The "cigar" float, (above) is clipped to the line, setting the minnow at a fixed depth. A slip bobber, (above right) slides up and down the line. A stop determines the depth and the minnow returns rapidly to the proper depth after each cast.

have vibrant colors, unblemished skin and fins, and tend to cluster in the holding tank. Diseased minnows usually are much darker than healthy ones, often have damaged skin and fins, and tend to school more loosely, with individuals often swimming listlessly near the surface. Confine your purchases to shops that keep their bait in good condition. Sick minnows will usually die before you reach your destination.

After obtaining minnows, you must do several things to keep them lively.

First, avoid extreme temperatures and sudden temperature changes. A bag or bucket full of minnows placed on ice may be full of belly-up bait in minutes. Dumping minnows into water that is significantly warmer or colder also may cause sudden death. Temper the fish by allowing their water to warm or cool gradually. Slowly add small amounts of water from your storage container or the body of water you're fishing until the temperature regulates. Then keep the baitfish cool but not cold. A temperature between 50 and 65 degrees is usually optimum. High temperatures kill minnows as quickly as cold.

It's also best to use unchlorinated water. This can be obtained from the water you're fishing or from a well or rain water. If tap water must be added, let the water stand overnight so the chlorine evaporates, or add dechlorinating tablets or drops. Additives can also be mixed with the water to keep ammonia and other harmful byproducts at acceptable levels.

Keeping the water well oxygenated is also important, especially if you need to keep the bait more than a few hours. You can accomplish this using products made to assist in this re-

It's important for minnows to be kept cool so they remain lively. The author uses a Coleman Xtreme Cooler with a towel-covered layer of cracked ice on the bottom for this purpose. Minnows placed in the cooler in bags can be kept this way for up to a week, even during hot weather.

gard, including aerators, trolling buckets and special livewells and tanks.

Finally, avoid overcrowding minnows, another cause of stress and death. Generally, one gallon of water will support 12 to 24 small to medium minnows. Minnows are often graded and sold by size, so take this into consideration when you make your purchase.

My method for keeping minnows lively is as follows:

First, I keep the minnows in the water my bait seller puts in the bags of minnows I buy. This water has chemicals that help keep the minnows lively.

Second, I ask the bait seller to add oxygen to each bag. Most bait shop operators can do this, and minnows will live much longer this way.

Third, I place the bag(s) of minnows in a Coleman Xtreme cooler that keeps ice three days or more, even in 90-degree weather. Beforehand, I add a layer of crushed ice a couple inches thick to the bottom of the cooler, then cover the ice with a

MINNOW TIPS

- When crappie seem persnickety, fish the outer edges of cover with no bobber on your rig. Without any weight except that of the hook and a small split shot, a minnow sinks very slowly, twisting and darting as it does. Crappie find such baits irresistible. You'll have to watch your line very closely as the bait sinks, looking for any slight movement indicating a hit. But when regular live bait tactics fail, this one can save the day.

- To fish minnows in and around wood cover, try this rig: Put a small bullet weight on your main line and tie a barrel swivel below it. Then tie a 4- to 6-inch leader (shorter leader in thicker brush) to the swivel, and a crappie hook to the leader. This rig is excellent for dropping a minnow through thick, small limbs. The minnow doesn't have a lot of free line for swimming to nearby limbs. When the sinker hangs, a quick twitch pulls it off the limb. When the hook snags, the sinker can be lowered to pull the hook free.

thick towel. The minnow bags are placed on top of the towel, the lid is shut and the temperature remains cool all day.

When I reach my fishing hole, I transfer the minnows and water from a bag into a styrofoam minnow bucket. If I expect to be on the water all day, I sometimes use a small, battery-powered aerator to insure the minnows have adequate aeration. I keep the minnow bucket inside my cooler so the temperature remains optimum.

Using this method, I've been able to keep minnows lively for several days.

Fishing With Minnows

Minnows can be fished using a variety of rigs and methods. They can be fished stationary or in motion under a cork. They can be tightlined. They can be trolled. They can be cast and retrieved. They can be used in combination with jigs. They can be rigged one at a time or in tandem. The ways in which you can employ minnows for crappie fishing are limited only by your imagination.

Some effective rigs are illustrated in the accompanying photos. A few basic principles should be observed when making them.

For example, it's best to use a fine-wired, long-shanked hook that won't injure the minnow as much as a heavier hook. Such a hook is also more easily removed from the crappie's mouth. Several styles can be used, but gold Aberdeen hooks are traditional favorites. Pick a size that's appropriate for the size of minnow being used: No. 4 to No. 1 for small to medium minnows, and up to 1/0 or 2/0 when using big minnows for trophy-class slabs.

Care should be used in hooking the minnow so it remains lively and stays on the hook. The lip-hook method probably works best overall, and is done simply by running the hook upward through the bottom lip and then the top lip. This method is used primarily when the minnow will be pulled through the water, either when trolling or using a cast/retrieve presentation. However, it works quite well for still fishing, too, even though most crappie anglers still prefer hooking the minnow through the back, just behind the dorsal fin, when using stationary presentations. "Eye-hooking" (running the hook through the upper portion of the eye sockets) is also common, but is more likely to kill the minnow.

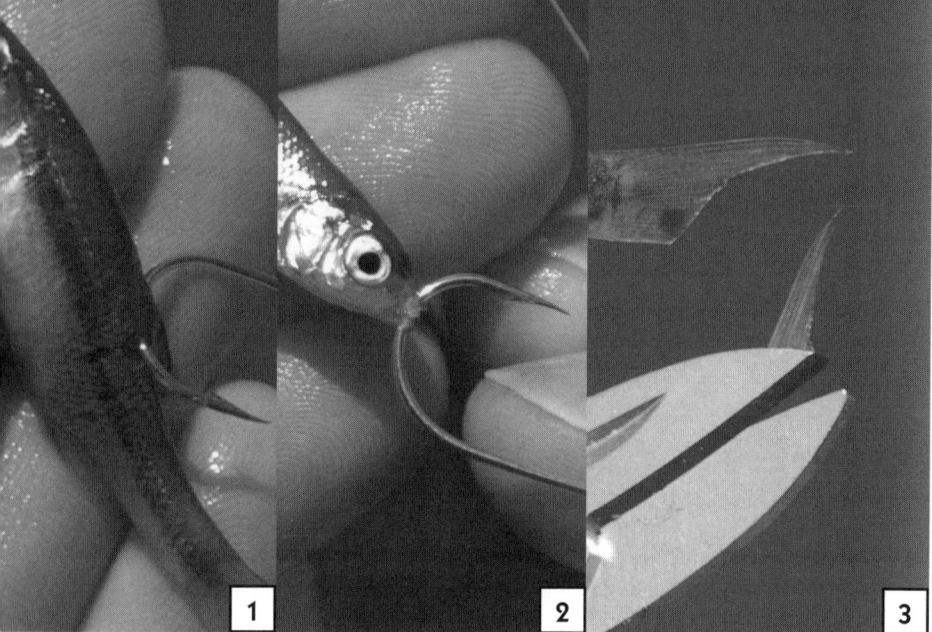

(1) Minnows typically are hooked near the dorsal fin for still fishing and (2) through the lips for trolling and casting. Light-wire hooks must be used to avoid killing the baitfish, and care should be taken not to pierce the minnow too deeply. (3) Snipping off a portion of a live minnow's tail makes the baitfish swim more erratically, thus attracting crappie that are on the lookout for an easy meal.

Rosy Red Minnows

Rosy red minnows, sometimes called pink minnows, are an unusual color strain of the fathead minnow. The name comes from the baitfish's reddish-orange hue, which closely resembles that of an orange goldfish.

Rosy reds were first propagated by fish farmer Billy Bland of Taylor, Arkansas. In the early 1980s, Bland began noticing a few orange fish in loads of black fatheads bought for his aquaculture operation. He hand-picked these rosy reds, placed them in a special rearing pond and eventually established a breeding population. Soon, he was producing rosy reds in quantity.

Bland's first big market was the "feeder" market. Rosy reds replaced freshwater guppies as the food of choice for many predatory aquarium fish. But before long, fishermen also heard about Bland's new minnow and coerced him to sell some for bait. Many of these anglers were crappie fishermen who knew that orange goldfish are relished by big slabs. They felt the rosy red's goldfish-like colors would also attract jumbo crappie.

They were right. Not only were rosy reds superb crappie bait, they frequently outproduced regular minnows. Bait dealers were soon inundated with orders for these new-fangled minnows. Their hardy nature made them especially popular with Northern ice fishermen. But other anglers were taking notice, too. Soon, rosy reds were available in 33 states.

Are rosy reds really better than golden shiners or other crappie minnows? Many anglers say yes.

Steve Filipek is an avid crappie fishermen and a fisheries biologist with the Arkansas Game & Fish Commission. He's been fishing with rosy reds for years. "My crappie catch has probably doubled since I started using them," he says. "I no longer feel comfortable using regular minnows."

Shad and other overlooked crappie catchers can often be caught using a cast net.

Overlooked Crappie Catchers

Can crappie be caught on natural baits other than minnows? Yes, but few live-bait anglers ever switch from minnows to other enticements because there's little need to. Ninety percent of the time, a hungry crappie will strike a shiner with little or no hesitation. During that other ten percent of the time, however, when crappie seem less enthusiastic about the bait you're presenting, you might want to consider these often-overlooked offerings.

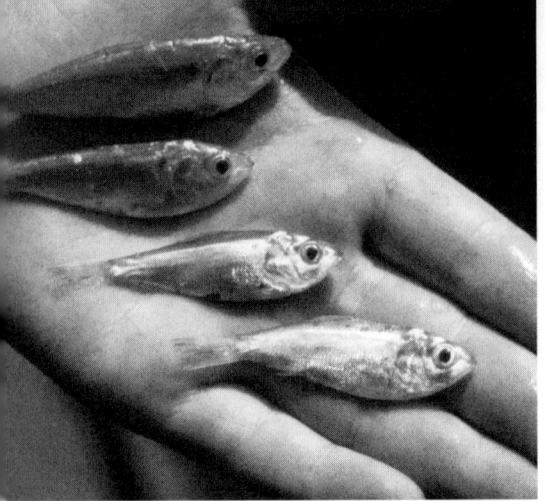

In many waters, threadfin shad comprise a large portion of the crappie's diet. Though hard to keep alive, these prolific fish make excellent baits when available.

Sunfish Fry

Young-of-the year sunfish are extraordinary baits at times. They work especially well in many ponds where sunfish fry make up the predominant food source of stocked crappie. They're fairly easy to obtain and store, hardy in almost any water temperature, super-lively on the hook, and, best of all, extra-appealing to big crappie.

Check your local regulations to determine the legality of using sunfish for bait. It's not permitted in some areas, and in others, there are limits on the size or species of sunfish you're allowed to use. To be on the safe side, know the laws governing collecting and using sunfish for bait. The same is true for the baitfish listed below.

Where laws permit it, one- to two-inch sunnies can be used to put crappie in the boat when all else fails. Sunfish are found in practically every body of water and often comprise a large portion of the crappie's forage base. Consequently, they're like candy to slab papermouths. They're wide-bodied, multicolored and easier for crappie to see in off-colored water, plus their constant frantic movements create fish-attracting vibrations that carry for long distances. The easier crappie can detect a bait, the more fish you're likely to put in your livewell.

A minnow seine, minnow trap or cast net are used to catch small sunfish, which can be stored in a minnow bucket. They're fished much like you'd fish minnows, but must be held farther from cover to keep them from showing their astounding talent for wrapping line around every stick. Fortunately, these struggles will coax crappie from cover they wouldn't leave for most baits.

The bait's normal movements feel almost like a crappie's gentle nip at a minnow. It takes practice to ignore those little taps and twitches, but there's no doubt when a nice crappie takes a sunfish; it strikes hard.

Shad

Shad, like small sunfish, often comprise a large portion of the crappie's diet, up to 50 to 90 percent of the total food intake in some waters. Yet, shad, too, seldom are considered when anglers select live bait for crappie fishing.

The two primary species of shad in our country are gizzard shad and threadfin shad. Small individuals of both species, up to 2 or 3 inches long, are relished by crappie.

Using a cast net is the most effective way to catch shad, but again, be sure to abide by regulations governing their collection and use. Where permitted, throw the net around bridges, piers or riprap where shad often school, and store your resulting catch in a large, well-insulated, aerated tank with stream or lake water, or rig a perforated garbage can to carry them alongside your boat. Shad are sensitive and die very easily, so don't overcrowd them. A gallon of water will support six to eight small shad.

Shad are very oily and impart a strong crappie-attracting scent to the water. They also have a flashy silver color. Both these characteristics make them especially good bait to use in dingy water where poor visibility hinders the crappie's ability to easily find more traditional baits. Rig them as you would a minnow "hooked through the lips or just under the dorsal fin" then work them around prospective hotspots. A bobber may be helpful under some conditions, but I've found one of the most effective rigs to be simply a crippled or just-deceased shad impaled on a hook and allowed to flutter to the bottom without any weight or float. In crappie-populated dam tailwaters, this is a real killer, because it mimics a shad that's been injured when passing through gates or turbines.

Other natural baits you may want to consider are: 1. earthworms, 2. the catalpa worms (the caterpillar of the catalpa sphinx moth), 3. crayfish, and 4. crickets.

Goldfish

While sunfish fry and shad usually must be caught from the wild by crappie anglers, goldfish are readily available from

Chapter IV: Considering Bait 75

many bait dealers. Why more crappie anglers don't use them as bait, I don't know. They're extremely hardy, staying lively on a hook for long periods even in poor-quality water.

When I've used orange-colored goldfish for bait (bait goldfish can be black or brown as well), it seems to me they're more easy for crappie to see and thus more likely to be eaten, especially in turbid or deep waters where visibility is limited. Ask your bait dealer to cull them and provide only those two inches or less.

Goldfish tend to be considerably more expensive than minnows, and sometimes are illegal to use or hard to find. But when crappie turn their noses up at minnows, goldfish seem well worth the price. In addition, the crappie I catch on goldfish usually average a bit larger than the ones I catch on minnows, often over a pound apiece.

Other Baits

Though there's not a very high demand for them in crappie fishing circles, many other natural baits also can be used by innovative crappie anglers. I've used earthworms and crickets, for instance, to catch literally hundreds of crappie. Not intentionally, mind you, but while fishing for bluegills. Nevertheless, knowing that crappie are opportunistic feeders that take advantage of almost any invertebrate food source small enough to swallow could come in handy in a pinch if other baits are unavailable.

I had an uncle who frequently caught crappie using cockroaches he caught in a homemade trap. In Louisiana, fresh-

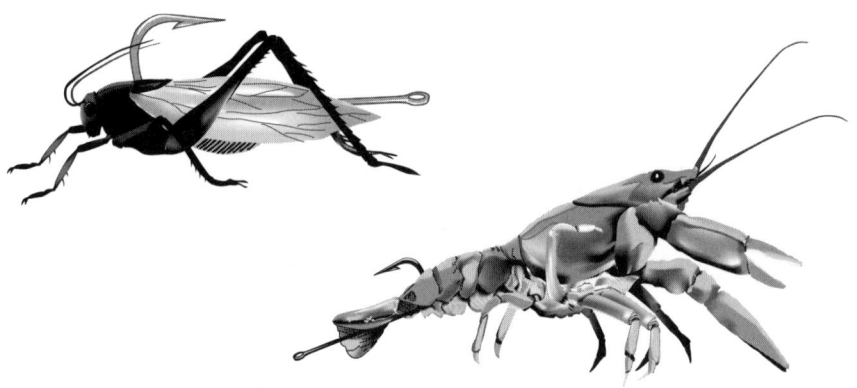

Hook a cricket (below) by inserting the point of the hook through the tail and running through the cricket, allowing the point to come out at the head. Live crawfish (below right) should be hooked through the back section of the tail.

water shrimp are a favorite bait for big "sac-a-laits." Catalpa worms, the caterpillars of catalpa sphinx moths, get a good bit of attention from Southern crappie fans, and in some northern waters, I'm told, tiny crawfish are local favorites for out-sized slabs.

If you were to talk with 100 ardent crappier anglers, there's little doubt you discover many other baits relished by papermouths as well. A few more I've heard about include dragonfly and damselfly larvae, scuds, wasp larvae, grasshoppers and maggots. There's not a conventional crappie-catcher among them, but I imagine each and every one would be snarfled up by a hungry crappie. Sometimes it pays to experiment to get the most from a fishing trip, and such baits might be good ones to try when all else fails.

Summer mayfly hatches are common on many crappie lakes, and when they occur, crappie move shallow to gorge on mayfly larvae and emerging adults. If you see numerous mayflies, dispense with lures and minnows, and try fishing an unweighted cricket instead. Although a cricket hardly resembles a mayfly, hungry crappie filling their bellies on insects won't refuse one. You could catch and use some of the mayflies that are swarming, but they're extremely delicate and hard to keep on the hook. Crickets work better. Hook the cricket through the collar to keep it lively, then flip it on top of the water and wait for the hit that is sure to come. You'll probably land as many bluegills as crappie, but where crappie are common, they'll comprise a good portion of your catch.

Tips for Overlooked Baits

- **Grass shrimp are excellent crappie baits.** Look for them in weedy bays and backwaters of delta rivers and oxbow lakes. A dip net or tight-meshed seine pulled through thick beds of water plants will often produce a significant amount on a single pass. Store them in a small container kept in a refrigerator or other cool place.

- **Crappie often lurk beneath lily pads, and baits can be found there.** Small aquatic invertebrates such as dragonfly and mayfly nymphs, grubs and worms often cling to the underside of the leaves. Scrape a few into a container with a little water, and fish them on a fine-wire hook. As part of the diet of local fish, they may outproduce conventional baits.

Chapter V

CRAPPIE SEASONS

SPRING: Crappie On the Beds

Crappie invade shallow-water haunts along the banks of lakes, rivers and ponds during the spring spawning season. This makes them much easier to find and catch than during other seasons, and results in more anglers fishing for crappie during this period.

During the week or two just prior to the actual spawn, male and female crappie go through sort of a feeding frenzy to offset their reproductive growth spurt. They're also trying to add energy reserves for the stressful spawning period when activity increases. Consequently, crappie are feeding more, and this is a good time to catch fish.

Another fact in the angler's favor is the concentration of fish during the spawn. There may be dozens of nests in an area

Spring is a season of bounty for crappie anglers. When these panfish are in the shallows on their beds, it's often easy to catch dozens in a short period of time.

little bigger than a school bus. And there may be several beds this size along a 100-yard stretch of shoreline. Because crappie are horded up in the shallows, they're much simpler to find.

Male crappie vigorously defend their nests from egg predators or anything they perceive might be an egg eater. If an intruder gets too close, the defending male chases it, nipping and biting until it leaves the area.

Crappie anglers can turn this aggression into a fishing boon. Many crappie taken during this period strike the bait not because it represents a food item but because it has intruded into their nesting territory. Males protect the just-hatched fry and continue to fiercely attack anything that comes near the nest area. Therefore they remain unusually susceptible to baits and lures for a week or more after nesting activities end.

Know When and Where To Go

A clear understanding of factors that trigger crappie spawning activity is essential for successful spring fishing.

Water temperature is one primary key. Most experts quote a figure of 56 degrees as the temperature at which nesting activity begins. But the peak of spawning activity may not occur until the temperature climbs to 58 or 60 degrees.

The exact time when the water reaches this temperature may vary from year to year, from latitude to latitude, and from one body of water to another. It is important that the crappie angler determine when these ideal spawning temperatures are most

"In spring, when other anglers are pounding the bank, back off and fish in water that's eight to 15 feet deep. This is where the biggest females will be holding. Everybody else will be catching the smaller male crappie while you are catching big slab females."

--Kevin Rogers,
Crappie USA Classic qualifier six consecutive years

likely to occur and do some on-the-water investigation that will lead to a visit during the peak of nesting activities.

Looking at sunrise-sunset tables can be helpful. I learned this from Steve Wunderle who wrote the excellent guide, *New Techniques That Catch More Crappie*. In this book, Steve tells of a study done on Missouri's Table Rock Lake by fisheries biologist Dr. Fred Vasey. Vasey learned that "The first [crappie] nests to appear had an average of 13.2 daylight hours," and "The last nesting sites occurred when the daylight averaged 14.6 hours." In other words, you can determine when the spawn is likely to begin and end, and therefore postulate when it might peak, by calculating the number of hours between sunrise and sunset on a given day. Abrupt changes in the weather influence this, particularly late cold fronts. But during years of "normal" weather, this has proven an excellent way to determine prime fishing days.

Also remember that crappie almost invariably nest in shallow coves protected from wind and wave action. Finding areas with these characteristics is the key to finding crappie beds. Nests are often near a log or other large object over a bottom of sand, fine gravel or interwoven plant roots. The depth at which nests are found can vary considerably, from less than one foot to as much as 20 feet. But most will be in one to five feet of water.

Additional Facts

Several nuances of the spawn may not be apparent until you've done further studying. One is the fact that the biggest crappie will often be in deeper water during the period when smaller males are first preparing nest sites. For this reason, it's a good idea to sometimes fish deeper areas away from shallow-water beds. Crappie weighing a pound and up have been around long enough to be considerably more wary than their young counterparts. And finding these angler-shy slabs may require fishing in water 7 to 15 feet deep, something few fishermen consider when there are so many nice fish found on shoreline beds.

Spawning activity is spread out over a period of time. Female crappie don't all become ripe at the same time, and the eggs from a single fish may mature gradually. An individual female may deposit eggs in batches over a period of two weeks or more. This assures at least some successful reproduction. Crappie will use the same spawning grounds continuously unless there is a major disturbance, so you can go back to the same beds time and time again during the spawn and still catch fish.

Current and often-changing water conditions can make river fishing tough, but big lowland rivers often produce big stringers of crappie for anglers savvy to the ways of moving-water panfish.

River Tactics for the Spawn

Rivers. Crappie. To most crappie anglers, these two words are totally unrelated. Crappie are considered lake fish, and when planning a crappie-fishing junket, rivers receive little attention.

If you were to live in a land of rivers and few lakes, however, you might think again about fishing flowing waters. Such was the case with Bill Peace of Jonesboro, Arkansas. Growing up in the lake-poor Delta of northeast Arkansas in the 1940s and '50s, Peace began his crappie-fishing career on big bottomland rivers like the Black, St. Francis and White. Today, there are several excellent crappie lakes near his home. But often as not, when it's crappie he's after, Peace returns to fish the rivers of his childhood.

"I started crappie fishing when I was just a boy," says Peace. "Back then, lakes were scarce in northeast Arkansas, so we fished the rivers. I discovered early on just how good river fishing can be, and though I often fish lakes nowadays, it's river fishing I enjoy most. It's a different, more challenging way of crappie fishing. But when it's good, it's the best there is. There are times when we catch 50 crappie an hour, and a lot of those will be big—a pound to three pounds each."

The best crappie rivers, according to Peace, are warm lowland rivers meandering through rich bottomland soils. If a river is cold enough for trout, or cool enough for smallmouth bass, it's not likely to hold many crappie, he notes. Bottomland rivers, on the other hand, often support phenomenal crappie populations.

"Some crappie fishermen never fish rivers," Peace says. "That's a big oversight. River fishing can be outstanding if you know how to do it."

Seasonal Considerations

River crappie are transients, moving from one area to another as seasons change. In summer and winter, extremes of heat and cold drive them to deep-water haunts, often in or near the main river channel. Spring and autumn offer more moderate water temperatures, allowing crappie to invade shallow, off-channel areas. During these seasons, they're often found in backwaters and other areas where current is inappreciable.

"If you know where to look for them, you can catch river crappie year-round," says Peace. "But the spring spawning season offers the best fishing. Crappie are in shallow areas then, and easier to find. They're more aggressive than they will be during fall."

Pinpointing River Crappie

Crappie rarely spawn in the main channel of a river. Most make their nests in backwater areas out of the current.

"In spring, the best crappie fishing is in still waters off the main river," says Peace. Look for big backwaters, side channels, places where current is reduced. Crappie prefer to spawn where they don't have to fight the current."

The areas Peace seeks have three

Fertile delta river systems often produce enormous crappie. During the spawn, most are caught from shallow backwaters and other areas where current is minimal.

The savvy river angler pays close attention to changing water levels in the river being fished. The rate of change often determines how good the crappie fishing will be.

important qualities: abundant cover, proper water temperature and stable water levels.

"River crappie usually nest where there's dense cover," he says. "Roughfish eat their eggs given the chance, so crappie get as far as they can back in brush tops, willows, stickups and other thick woody cover. When you're trying to find a good fishing area, start by looking for heavy cover in shallow areas off the main river.

"The second thing to look for is warm water," he continues. "Crappie begin spawning activities in water that's 56 degrees, and they'll move out of cooler water as soon as they can. The thing is, water temperature isn't the same everywhere in a river. It fluctuates from one spot to another, and that can make it tough to find fish. Crappie may move out of the main river and into a warmer tributary. Or they may move to water that's a little muddier, because silty water warms quicker than clear water. It's important to find areas with the proper water temperature in order to find fish."

Fluctuating water levels also affect crappie behavior. And most big bottomland rivers are subject to extreme fluctuations during spring.

"Good river anglers keep track of changing water levels in the newspaper or through other sources," says Peace. "What you want to check is the rate of change. If a river is rising fast or falling fast, crappie fishing won't be good, even in backwater areas. The fish just quit biting. The best fishing is when there's a slow rate of change or no change at all, so try to plan your trip when the river's stable."

Establishing a Pattern

Being a successful river angler requires flexibility, Peace says. In other words, crappie anglers must be willing to change lures, tactics and locations as often as necessary to establish a fishing pattern.

"Lure color is a good example," Peace notes. "In the backwater areas I usually fish, crappie almost always hit a red jig with a chartreuse tail. If that doesn't work, a jig that's red-and-white or blue-and-white usually will.

"There are times, though, when my favorite colors just won't work. So I keep changing until I find something crappie will bite on that particular day under those particular conditions."

Anglers may also have to vary their presentation.

"You may have to raise and lower the jig as you're fishing," Peace says. "Or you may have to hold it completely still and watch for your line to go slack when a crappie hits. One day they like one presentation, the next day they may prefer another.

"The key to catching river crappie is establishing a pattern. Do they want jigs or minnows? If jigs, what color? Should I jig the lure or hold it stationary? Are they in willow thickets or brushy tops? We may be the best crappie fishermen in the world and go out and not catch a fish. On the same day at the same place, a novice may go out and load his boat with fish. The difference is, the novice was able to establish a pattern. You've got to find that pattern. That's the key."

Does Peace have favorite fishing spots on the rivers he fishes?

"Everybody has favorite places to fish," he says. "I usually fish on the lower end of the White River just above its confluence with the Mississippi. In that area, secondary willows are among the best crappie fishing places. These are willows growing out into a backwater as the backwater silts in. The water moves up and then down, year after year, depositing more silt. And as the silt piles up, the willows take hold farther and farther out from the bank. Fishing the outermost willows in these areas can produce lots of big crappie.

"I'm continually on the lookout for new fishing areas, too," Peace continues. "When the water's high and muddy, and fishing isn't too good, I'll do some scouting. High water lets you get back into chutes, cuts and backwaters off the river, places you may not have noticed before. And while you're up in these areas, you may find that water off the main river is clearer and easier to fish. If you find the right spot, it could turn a bad fishing day into a good one. At the very least, you should find new places to try when water conditions are more favorable."

Willows growing away from the bank often hold schools of heavyweight river-system crappie.

Is river fishing really that different than lake fishing? After reviewing Peace's suggestions, you may think not.

"The basics of crappie fishing are the same whether you're fishing a little lake or a big river," says Peace. "But fishing rivers and fishing lakes is teetotally different. You need to fish a river quite a bit to know exactly how and where to fish. You have to practice at it. River crappie are more aggressive because they've had to battle currents all their life. But they're more finicky, too, more likely to move around and change their behavior patterns. That makes river fishing tough.

"That doesn't mean you shouldn't try it, though. There have been times, especially during the spawn, when I've limited out in 45 minutes. River crappie tend to gather in large groups in very small areas, and if you get on a pattern, you can tear them up.

"Lake fishing is fun in its own right," Peace concludes. "But if you want to experience the most exciting and most challenging form of crappie fishing, rivers are where it's at."

Post-Spawn Fishing for River Crappie

After spawning, river crappie remain in off-channel areas until summer's heat warms the water to near the 80° mark. At this time crappie migrate back to cooler, oxygenated water in the deeper main river channel.

"Catching summer crappie isn't hard," says Bill Peace. "But you must be able to pinpoint specific areas in the main river where crappie are likely to hold.

"Most crappie will be near current breaks like logs, willow thickets or rock wing dikes that have brushy cover around them. Fighting current is a waste of energy, so they try to find areas where current is reduced. You'll need to use bigger jigs in this situation and be prepared to get hung up some because of the current."

Peace suggests positioning your boat close to the structure you want to fish, then work the structure thoroughly. "A single spot may hold a dozen or more big slabs," he says. "Don't leave too soon."

Polarized sunglasses provide a definite advantage for sight fishing crappie anglers by cutting glare off the water.

Sight Fishing for Spring Slabs

Spring rains have fallen steadily for days, but finally, we get a break in the weather. When we slide my johnboat in the oxbow, the rising sun shines brightly through the cypress trees.

I scull the boat to lake's upper end while my fishing partner ties a jig to the line on a long pole and slides into his waders. The boat serves merely to transport us from the ramp to flooded woods on the oxbow's far side. Today, we'll be wade fishing.

We both realize this is a hit-or-miss situation. All conditions—water temperature, day length and other factors—must be perfect for us to succeed. Sometimes we time it right; other

The sharp-eyed angler may be able to see crappie and cast to individual fish when schools move shallow to spawn.

times we fail. But when all is good, we come to this seldom-fished lake and find crappie spawning in astounding numbers.

Fortunately for us, on this day, everything is perfect. The rising lake has inundated the low-lying woods along its edge. The water temperature is just right. As soon as we start wading, we see them.

The water they are in is just inches deep. In most places, it is not enough to hide the crappie's protruding dorsal fins. Even where it is, we still can see swirls the fish make as they move in the shallows.

A flip of the line places my buddy's tube jig beside one swirl. Immediately, a crappie nabs the lure. The jig pole arcs as my friend lifts the crappie, removes the hook and places the speckled panfish in the floating fish basket tied to his waist.

I've chosen a different tactic—pitching a Crappie Slider rigged on an ultralight spinning outfit. This proves equally effective. I cast to one fin and barely move the lure when a crappie strikes. It's a dandy, but when I reach down to lip it, the fish thrashes and gets away.

Not to worry, though. I'll have more chances. I can see crappie in every direction.

After an hour of fishing, my fish basket is heavy. When I reach the boat, my partner is finishing his count. "Twenty-one, twenty-two, twenty-three ... twenty-three crappie. Not too bad, huh?"

I had twenty-two.

Many anglers employ sight fishing to catch their favored quarry. In pools of clear mountain streams, fly fishermen see trout profiles and place their lures within slurping distance. From a bass boat's bow, an angler casts to spawning largemouths in the shallows. In a johnboat, a fisherman watches for the telltale "honeycombs" of bluegill nests.

Sight fishing for crappie, however, remains a seldom-used tactic.

To some extent, the crappie's cover-loving nature accounts for the lack of participants. Unlike bass and bluegills, which often nest on open bottom where they are easily seen, crappie prefer bedding sites in flooded vegetation or waters thick with brush, logs, stumps and other dead-wood cover. Sight fishing in these areas seems as ludicrous as star gazing on a cloudy night.

The crappie's superb camouflage also makes it a difficult sight-fishing target. This fish is invisible to all but the keenest eyes, and you can't sight fish for quarry you cannot see.

Consider as well that crappie often spawn in relatively deep water. Beds in 10-20 feet of water are not unusual in clear lakes. Combine this with the fact that crappie have rather poorly defined nests, and the difficulties are further compounded. Even in crystal-clear water, these fish and their beds can be difficult to see.

At times, however, sight fishing for crappie can prove quite productive, particularly during the peak of the spring spawning season. The operative word here is "peak." Laying eyes on a crappie is troublesome at best before and after the period when fish are building or guarding their nests. But for several weeks each spring, crappie enter that shallow-water world between dry land and deep water, and if you know what to look for, you can use your eyes to zero in on individual bedding fish and catch them.

Finding the Best Sight Fishing Locales

If you've fished a body of water before, and know the location of previous crappie bedding sites, return to those areas. Crappie tend to nest in the same locales year after year.

If this is your first visit, look at a good bottom contour map to pinpoint likely hotspots. Look for places where creek channels approach the shore. Crappie follow channels from deep water to shallow, and tend to spread out on either side of the channel/spawning cover junction if conditions are suitable. Shallow water in the backs of feeder creek bays often prove good as well. Look, too, for visible migration corridors that lead to shallow-water cover—stump rows, old fence lines, weed lines, ditches and the like. The key combination is shallow water with abundant cover and a firm, not silty, bottom.

The best sight fishing locales, in my experience, are woodlands and brushy areas temporarily flooded by high water. These spots may not exist unless heavy rainfall or other conditions have created them. They may never exist on some upland impoundments. They occur with some regularity, however, on oxbow lakes and occasionally on impoundments subject to high water levels during rainy springs.

When high water inundates shallow woodlands or brush, crappie often leave traditional spawning sites and nest instead in the shallow, food-filled waters that now exist. Here, they are much more visible to the astute angler. Often as not, you'll find them in the shallowest areas at the edge of the high-water pool where they're quite easy to see. In most cases, the best way to reach these areas is by wading. In some situations, however, you may be able to work a boat close enough to fish the beds.

Tactics

Wear polarized sunglasses when sight fishing. They reduce glare on the water and enable you to better see the fish. You'll see twice as many crappie with polarized glasses as you would without.

There are two things you may see that will tip you off to the location of each individual fish: the actual fish, or water movement –a swirl, splash or wake—made by the fish.

In the former case, you may see only part of the fish—a fin or tail protruding from the water, for example. Or all you may spy is a shadowy figure hovering over the bottom. A crappie that's not moving is almost invisible, even in clear water. But with time, you'll learn how to discern a crappie from its surroundings.

Most often you'll only see signs that a crappie is present. Perhaps it will be a shallow wake as a male guarding a nest darts out to chase away an intruder. Or it could be the telltale disturbance on the water's surface as a crappie rises to gobble an insect or passing minnow.

Stop when you spy the first fish and scan each side and all around to see if you can spot other crappie. On a good bed, the fins of a dozen or more fish may be visible. Knowing where the fish are helps determine which ones you should target first so you don't spook some away unnecessarily.

When fish are pinpointed, present a bait or lure right on the spot. Some anglers prefer a long jigging pole to swing a jig or minnow to each fish. Others prefer using a spinning or spincast outfit to work the bait from a greater distance.

One of my favorite setups is a Charlie Brewer Weedless Crappie Slider fished with ultralight tackle. Because it's relatively weedless, I can cast and retrieve this lure without worry of hangups. I place the slider just beyond the spot where I see a fish, then bring it back past the fish. Small floating crankbaits work well using this tactic, too. Productive models include Rebel's Super Teeny-R and ¼-ounce Humpback; Cabela's 1-

inch, $1/16$-ounce Micro; Rapala's 2-inch Shallow Shad Rap; and Mann's Tiny One-Minus. Jig/spinner combos like Johnson's Beetle Spin also work well.

If the water is clear but nests are in brushy areas or weed beds, I use a jigging pole and try to place a minnow or jig on top of the fish I see. It's best to stand so you can see better, but wear a lifejacket in case you take a tumble. Look into every nook and cranny in the cover for crappie hovering over their nests. Then work the bait back to the fish and lower it quietly into the water. No movement of your enticement is necessary. If the crappie is in a feeding mood or actively guarding the nest, a strike will come quickly.

Occasionally you'll see clusters of crappie nests on shallow gravel bars or other open structures, particularly in waters with little brushy cover. Most will be near logs, stumps or other cover objects, and though the crappie themselves may not be readily visible, casting a minnow, jig, small crankbait or other crappie-catcher to a nest quickly will determine if crappie are there.

In this and other clear-water situations, it may help to suspend minnows or jigs beneath a small clear bobber. An enticement dangled at the crappie's eye level rather than on the bottom often produces better. Try fishing minnows without adding a sinker or swivels. This, too, may increase your number of hookups.

Wade fishing is a good way to find crappie in shallow flooded woodlands.

Working small diving crankbaits on points is a good way to nail big spring crappie.

Spring Fishing Tips

Almost anyone can catch crappie when they're bedding in the shallows. The following tips, however, will improve your fishing success throughout the spring—before, during and after the spawn.

Watch the Weather

Successful prespawn anglers know how crappie react to changing weather patterns. This season has lots of bumps, starts and backups. Warming trends are interrupted by sudden cold fronts. Crappie migrate from deep water to shallow and back several times before settling into spawning patterns.

The best fishing usually is toward the end of warm spells. One clue is a cold front approaching after several warm days. During this time, male crappie start fanning in shallows. Females also move shallow, looking for food. Therefore, focus fishing efforts on shallow waters where spawning will occur.

When a cold front hits, crappie return to deeper waters, holding near distinct bottom structure where light penetration is minimal and winter cover is abundant. If conditions are sunny and windy (typical after a cold front arrives), wave action cuts light penetration, and crappie remain near mid-depth structure. Several days after the cold front hits, the wind calms, allowing greater light penetration and driving crappie to deeper structure and cover.

If weather remains sunny and begins warming before the passage of another cold front, crappie gradually begin migrating back to shallow waters. Rainy weather, especially a warm rain, sends them scurrying to shallow reaches.

I've seen crappie have a drastic mood swing literally overnight when spring cold fronts descend, lowering surface temperatures with bone-chilling winds. Crappie relate close to structure in this scenario. Slow down your presentation to a vertical style, keeping the bait in front of the fish longer and in their specific depth range. Don't expect the fish to be aggressive and chase down a moving bait, as they're tight in the structure. Light or small lure sizes will help too, as will using a bobber for slow, sinking presentations that assist you in keeping the bait in the strike zone longer.

A sudden Spring cold snap can cause crappie to hang close to underwater structures. A slow presentation at a fixed depth works well in this situation.

Consider all these factors when selecting areas in which to focus your fishing efforts.

Points & Crankbaits

During the earliest part of pre-spawn, crappie often hold on points sloping toward bottom channels. Among the best lures for fishing these areas are small, deep-diving, baitfish-imitating crankbaits.

When spring weather turns rainy, crappie often move from deep to shallow water, making them easier to find and catch.

It's difficult to keep crankbaits at favored depths and still move them slow enough to entice lethargic crappie. Using a neutral buoyancy or sinking crankbait eliminates these problems. Use light line (4- to 6-pound-test), crank the lure down to the proper depth and then slowly crawl it across the bottom.

Fish crankbaits around cover on each point, retrieving the lure from shallow water to deep, or working across the point toward the deepest side. Crappie move up and down points as weather and water conditions change and may be difficult to pinpoint. But when the first fish is found, you might take several on consecutive casts.

The best points to fish drop quickly into deep water. You must crank your lure hard and fast several turns to get it near bottom before slowing to an effective pace. If possible, bump the lure against stumps, logs, boulders, etc. to elicit strikes. If no cover is around, walk the lure along the lake floor, nicking the bottom. A crankbait with a big lip will roll on its side when contact is made, and this is usually when a crappie nails it.

Try Tailwaters

Don't overlook the opportunity to take loads of spring crappie in the tailwater below a big-river dam. River crappie often move upstream in early spring, searching for spawning sites. When they reach a dam, they mill around for a while, and you have an excellent chance for extraordinary catches. A jig/minnow combination often outproduces a jig or minnow alone in this situation. Cast around wing dams, boulders, lock walls and other current breaks where crappie can rest and feed.

Remember Hotspots

As crappie are caught and removed from a spawning bed, other fish move in to take over prime nesting sites. Therefore, fishing may continue to be good at a single site for many days throughout the spawn.

Pinpoint the Right Depth

Crappie spawn deeper in clear water and shallower in murky water. To pinpoint the depth where they're most likely to be nesting, make a version of the scientist's Secchi disk. Cut an 8-inch circle from a piece of sheet metal and paint it white. Drill a hole in the circle's center and attach an eyebolt there. Tie a nylon cord to the bolt and lower the disk into the water on the shady side of your boat. Don't wear sunglasses. The depth of most nests will be the same depth where the disk disappears from view.

An Inconspicuous Marker

Crappie on beds often get spooked and disappear. If you wait 15 or 20 minutes and come back, chances are the fish will be in the same spot. But if you use an ordinary marker buoy to mark the spot, someone else is likely to see it and beat you to the punch. Instead, tie a piece of brightly colored yarn around a stickup or weed stem near the bedding area. That way, only you will know the location of the hotspot.

Return to Deeper Water

Spawning may continue until the water temperature reaches 70 degrees or more. As soon as crappie leave their beds and shallow-water fishing takes a nosedive, look for fish in the same staging areas where they were found just prior to the spawn, places such as points, creek channel edges and dropoffs bordering shallow flats.

Some crappie anglers quit fishing after the spawn, but summer is a season of plenty too, if you know where to look for crappie and how to entice them.

SUMMER: Dog Days Fillets

It was a typical "dog days" afternoon—fiery and humid with only an occasional breeze to bring relief. For several hours, bluegill fishing on the oxbow lake was outstanding. But as the chuck-wills-widows started their evening roundelay, the bream fishing tapered off.

Plop. The bobber twisted and settled. No takers. Move to the next spot. Plop, twist, settle. Wait. Still nothing. We maneuvered our crickets in, over, under, through and around every piece of cover, but no amount of wheedling could rouse another strike.

I decided a last-ditch effort for bass was in order. A barn

swallow skimmed the water's surface as I tied the boat to a tall mid-lake snag. I'd seen two men sink a big cedar there two months earlier.

A baitcasting rod was put into play, and for the next 30 minutes, I plied the brush pile with a variety of lures. Nothing. Switching to an ultralight spinning combo, I tied on a tiny chartreuse tube jig, tipped it with a lively minnow and cast out near the sunken tree. Maybe the big guys wouldn't bite, but perhaps I could entice a couple of little ones.

The next hour was unforgettable. Not for the glorious rose-and-amber sunset that capped the day. Not even for the river otter I saw playing across the lake. On the first cast, I hooked a pound-and-a-half crappie, and there were 20 thrashing in the ice chest within the hour. None was a real "barn door," but several rated at least a "Wow!"

This fishing trip, and others like it, have convinced me to pursue crappie more often during summer. Granted, catching these feisty panfish isn't as easy in summer as during the spring spawn when crappie are concentrated in the shallows. But for the angler who knows where, when and how, the rewards of summer crappie fishing are many.

The first rule of summer crappie fishing is keying in on deeper water areas outside the normal realm of shallow-water anglers. Despite the fact that they're often moving, that's where most crappie hang out on a regular basis.

Concentrate your search in the 10- to 25-foot range. The clearer the water, the deeper you should look. Crappie are usually near woody cover along the edges of inundated stream channels, points and turns on weed edges, rock piles rising into well-oxygenated water, man-made fish attractors and other structure-oriented cover.

In waters with plentiful cover, the trick is finding the small percentage of it that holds fish. You may have to work hard to locate a concentration of crappie. Where cover is in short supply, a single sunken treetop may harbor dozens of slabs, but you must find that spot first.

Some deep-water crappie are found using hit-and-miss tactics like drift-fishing and trolling. But if you want to increase your hooking time and decrease your looking time, buy a good sonar fish finder. Electronic hardware is essential to find deep-water crappie consistently. Deep water, even water no deeper than the length of your boat, can hide a lot.

For example, it's one thing to know that a river channel zigzags through a long narrow cove. It's quite another to find a bend, ledge or some other nuance on the channel that will attract a school of crappie. Without sonar, you might never find such an area. But with a serious look at a bottom contour map and a quick check of prominent bottom changes with sonar, you could be catching slabs in minutes.

On lakes that stratify during summer, it's even easier to narrow down the waters where crappie are found. Stratified lakes have a layer of cool, unoxygenated water on the bottom and a layer of hot, oxygen-rich water on top. A layer of fairly cool, oxygen-rich water called the thermocline is sandwiched between the two. Regardless of whether the thermocline is eight inches thick or eight feet thick, that's probably where you'll find crappie.

The depth of the thermocline varies from lake to lake. To find it, keep an eye on your sonar while moving around the lake, and look for suspended fish. You'll notice that most are about the same depth. That's the thermocline, or at least the depth zone you're looking for. When fishing, start at that depth.

If you don't have sonar, try drifting or trolling. Rig your poles with minnows and/or different color jigs set at different depths. Then use the wind or your trolling motor to drift over prospective crappie-holding areas. Make a large zigzagging sweep that takes you past stump fields, weed edges and other types of cover in fairly deep water.

When you catch a crappie, change your rigs to conform to the fishes' bait and depth preferences, and toss out a marker buoy to pinpoint the location. Summer crappie are likely to be congregated in a fairly small area, and drifting a few yards either way could mean getting out of the action.

A common mistake is staying in one place too long. In summer, if crappie are present and feeding, they'll usually let you know right away. Contrary to popular belief, the dog days are not a period of sluggishness. A high summer metabolic rate means crappie are frequently feeding, and heavy schooling creates competitive group activity. If you aren't catching fish within 15 minutes, try another spot.

Lightweight, sensitive fishing equipment is a must for light-biting summer crappie. A good ultralight spinning outfit or graphite jigging pole works great if it has a soft, sensitive tip. This allows you to lift up slightly and watch for the slightest bend in the tip that indicates a fish has taken your bait. Watch your line for a slight twitch or slackening that signals a hit.

Jigs and minnows, or jig/minnow combos, are the preferred baits of most anglers, but don't overlook other possibilities. Small spoons, deep-diving crankbaits and spinners are also productive. Four-pound line works well in most situations, but you may want to switch to 6-pound or heavier when fishing heavy brush.

If you put your crappie pole in storage after the spawning season, get it out again. Remember, summer crappie aren't hard to catch, they're just a little harder to find. When you've zeroed in on a hot-weather slab hideout, likely as not you can stay in one place and catch enough to feed your family—maybe enough to feed the next-door neighbors, too. The dog days are crappie days, despite what you may hear.

> **Pro Tip**
>
> "When fishing shallow water, especially when flipping or shooting docks, give the good old corks a try. When you locate the depth where crappie are holding, you can set the cork, and therefore keep the jig in the strike zone. Many times, without a cork, the jig may only be in the strike zone for a short time during your retrieve. With the cork, it keeps the jig in the strike zone the entire time. It also allows you to slow down your presentation. Many times the fish will strike after you give the jig a small twitch and then let the jig stand still.
>
> "When using a cork, always try to use one just big enough to hold up the size jig that you are using. For this technique, many times a 1/48 oz. jig head is all you need, and this will allow you to use a very small cork. The fish will feel very little resistance."
>
> --Russ Bailey, www.midwestcrappie.com

When summer temperatures peak, crappie often feed more actively at night, and anglers who plans their after-hours junkets properly may catch dozens of good-eating slabs.

Crappie at Night

For many anglers, summer crappie fishing conjures up memories of the whip-poor-will's call and starlit nights. You can catch hot-season crappie during daylight hours, especially during cloudy periods or when water is muddy. But the odds of success improve if you fish the hours between dusk and dawn. During summer, many crappie work the late shift, and crappie anglers should, too.

These ten tips can help make your next nighttime outing for slabs a success.

Plan For Action

Thorough pre-trip planning can spell the difference between a good night-fishing trip and a bad one.

First, plan where you'll fish. The best night-fishing lakes are generally deep, fairly clear and exceed 500 acres. They're fertile, support abundant baitfish and have a good mix of structure and cover with areas of open water adjacent to structural elements.

In small, shallow waters, summer crappie fishing is generally poor. Crappie have no cool, oxygen-rich depths to which they can retreat. If water conditions are really bad, they become semi-dormant. They may scatter to conserve oxygen. Fishing suffers.

Fishing from a lighted dock produced this nice mess of crappie for the author.

Picking a good lake using these guidelines isn't foolproof. But by coupling this information with a few questions to the right individuals (state fisheries personnel, crappie anglers, tackle shop owners, etc.), you can narrow the field to a few choice waters.

You also should plan for the unique conditions encountered when night-fishing. Make sure running lights on your boat are working properly. Carry a flashlight or spotlight to signal your presence to other boats. Wear a lifejacket and kill switch.

Organize gear before leaving home. Clean out unnecessary equipment. Have poles rigged and ready to go. Organize your tacklebox. Recharge batteries for sealed-beam lights. Carry extra lantern fuel and mantles, anchors with an adequate length of rope to hold your boat stationary, marker buoys to pinpoint fishing holes and insect repellent.

Plot The Right Spot

Know exactly where you'll fish when darkness falls. Prospect during daylight hours, and be sure you can find each fishing spot after nightfall if you leave and return. Select alternate sites in case of a change in plans.

If possible, study a bottom-contour map of the lake. Most

hot-weather crappie congregate in deep, open water near breaklines (areas where there's a sudden change in depth on the lake bottom), so look for elevation markings indicating deep-water ledges, creek and river channels, points, ridges and humps.

The map directs you to a likely position, then a sonar unit pinpoints breaklines. The drop-offs are then checked with a graph or liquid-crystal unit to locate crappie-attracting cover (stumps, treetops, brushpiles, etc.) and the crappie themselves.

After spotting crappie on sonar, use buoys to mark the site. This enables you to fish in the most productive water without straying off.

Structure Your Success

As already noted, crappie in most prime summer lakes will be near deep underwater structure. Some structures, however, are better than others.

Inundated stream channels are among the best. Start at the mouth of a major tributary, then troll back and forth across the area, using sonar to follow the edge of the channel drop while looking for humps, points, bends, lines of timber and other structure that concentrates fish. Outside bends and junctions of two channels are blue-ribbon hotspots.

Summer crappie also orient to pilings and submerged riprap beneath bridges crossing deep water. With sonar, you can ease along the piers and spot fish concentrations while also pinpointing the depth of the fish. Without sonar, it's still a simple matter to pinpoint fish around bridge structures by fishing various depths and structures.

Bluffs and steep points also rate high for night-fishing. When moving from deep water to shallower reaches at night, crappie prefer sticking close to structures leading from one area to the other. It's like a blindfolded person grasping a string that serves as a guideline. Without the string, there's no reference point when moving around. Bluffs and points are crappie's after-dark guide lines and almost always prime night-fishing spots.

Although usually in shallow waters, lighted docks and marinas are also first-rate night-fishing spots. Overhead lights attract flying insects and baitfish, and many dock owners place crappie-attracting brushpiles nearby.

Follow The Fish

When fishing during early and late summer, track crappie's movements. Immediately after spawning, crappie usually are on structure leading from shallow bedding sites to deep-water summer haunts, structures like secondary stream channels and long sloping points. As summer wanes and day-length shortens, they make short forays between deep and shallow water, again using travel lanes like points, but also using shorter routes on humps, bluffs and other steep structure. In mid-summer, they'll be near the thermocline adjacent to deep structure.

Follow the fish. Know where they're likely to be when you start your search.

Many different types of crappie lights are available for the night fisherman. All can be helpful when fishing between dusk and dawn, but knowing how to use each correctly is necessary for success.

Use The Right Night Light

Some night-fishing anglers use only lanterns like the Coleman. Others use only sealed-beam lights. Smart anglers use both and use them correctly.

Hanging lanterns attract insects which attract baitfish which attract crappie. This isn't an instantaneous process, of course, so give it time to work.

Use at least two lanterns positioned on the same side of the boat so insects don't fog around your head. Hang them close to the water's surface from a boat-mounted bracket or tied to overhead objects. This provides light for tying knots, hooking bait and unhooking fish.

Sealed-beam crappie lights have a styrofoam flotation ring. They're an added attraction for fish but not bugs because the headlight-like beam points down in the water. The light helps concentrate baitfish and crappie. Power is from a pair of alligator clips to the battery or a cigarette-lighter plug. Position each light so you can fish in or around the beam.

Some models of crappie lights are made to sink beneath the water's surface and light up the depths below. These, too, are good additions to your night-fishing setup.

Black (ultraviolet) lights are another useful night-fishing aid.

They make fluorescent monofilament glow, allowing easy bite detection. Several models that run off 12-volt systems are available.

Two Rigs Are Better Than One

When you start fishing, it's hard to tell where crappie are in relation to your lights. Having several rigs in the water (where law permits) helps pinpoint them.

Place one rig near a light and others spaced along the length of the boat. Often the best area is near the light. At other times, crappie bite better on the fringes. This may indicate there's structure near the place they're biting and none where there's no action. Moving the lights or boat to get positioned more directly over the fish may help.

Get Down But Not Out

Until you determine the crappies' preference, set baits at different depths using water clarity as a guide. If the lake is clear, crappie may be at 20 to 30 feet; in stained water 10 to 20 feet, and in muddy water 5 to 10 feet. Remember, however, your lights will draw the fish closer to the surface. The key is to get your bait down to the level where fish are feeding but not beneath or above the strike zone. If you start with rigs at different depths, figuring the pattern is easier.

Look At Your Hook

The biggest mistake most crappie anglers make is using a hook that's too big or one with a strong, stiff shank. When these hang on branches or other cover, you disturb fish in the cover and may break your line trying to get unsnagged.

Light-wire hooks not only keep minnows alive and active, they also hook crappie firmly and can be straightened when they hang. Carry plenty of fine-wire Aberdeens in different sizes for a range of bait and crappie sizes.

Mark For The Dark

The biggest problem when night-fishing is seeing your equipment, but a can of fluorescent paint can be used to mark equipment for easy visibility. You'll be surprised how much easier it is to see a bright yellow bobber than a white one. A splotch of glowing paint in a tackle box compartment eliminates the painful experience of sorting hooks by Braille. A stripe of fluorescent color on black needle-nose pliers thwarts their usual invisibility.

Painting a black rod tip helps in detecting light biters.

The benefits are compounded when you use black lights. Look for special paints at craft stores that glow under ultraviolet.

Serve A Buffet

Jigs and minnows are the best crappie baits, day and night. But at times it pays to vary the menu for discriminating night-time diners.

If crappie are feeding on shad attracted to your lights, shad may outproduce minnows. Where legal, catch them with a dip net or cast net, then clip the tail or fins to give them an erratic, "crippled" action. Crappie can't resist.

Swarms of mayflies may be attracted to your lights. And at times, crappie gorge on the mayflies while refusing baitfish. Be watchful for such phenomena and act accordingly.

Among artificials, small jigging spoons and spinners compete with jigs. When allowed to fall on a slack line through schooling baitfish beneath your lights, they'll quickly garner a bite from opportunistic crappie.

In summer, crappie bite at night, everywhere they're found. The key to catching them is knowledge of their summer habits and versatility. If one location or tactic doesn't work, try another. If that doesn't work, try again. Sooner or later you'll discover the true joys night-fishing offers.

Spoons can be used to catch crappie year-round, but they're particularly effective in summer for taking crappie holding in deep water around standing timber.

Summer Fishing Tips

During hot weather, crappie fishing gets tough ... unless you know the secrets for summer success. These tips could help.

Try Bottom Fishing

When you know the thermocline's depth, look for areas where crappie-attracting structures cover the bottom at that depth, then bottom-fish a live minnow. Thread a slip sinker on your line, and below it, tie on a barrel swivel. To the swivel's lower eye, tie a 3-foot leader of light line tipped with a crappie hook. Add a minnow, then cast the rig and allow it to settle to the bottom. When a crappie takes the bait, the line moves freely through the sinker with no resistance to alert fish to a possible threat.

Attract Minnows, Attract Crappie

When fishing is slow during daylight hours, try an approach that duplicates the use of a crappie light at night. A light attracts insects, which in turn attracts minnows. But minnows also are attracted by chumming with dry dog food, bread crumbs or similar offerings. Scatter the chum by handfuls in several shallow-water areas, then move back to the first place you put chum and drop in a minnow. Fish each consecutive spot and see if your catch rate doesn't improve. Often, it will.

Scale Drop

Here's another "chumming" method to try when fishing is slow. Save some scales from the next crappie you dress. Rinse them and store inside a sealable container filled with water. Carry the container on your outings, and if things get slow, drop a few scales in the water above inundated cover. Crappie blow out the scales of baitfish as they eat them. As the scales fall, they flicker and catch the eye of crappie, which often will move toward them to investigate. A jig or minnow presented on a tight line in the vicinity of scales you drop may get hit.

On the Surface

Near dawn or dusk, summer crappie schools may surface to feed on minnows or shad. The attentive angler can zero in on such schools by watching for rough patches on an otherwise smooth lake surface. Use a trolling motor or paddle to approach barely within casting range. A long rod (six-feet-plus) and small spinning reel spooled with 2- to 4-pound test line allow longer casts with shad imitations such as jigs, spinners or live minnows. Suspend the lure or bait a few inches below a bobber, and get ready for action.

Cypress Water Tips

Cypress-shrouded lakes and bayous tend to be shallow, which allows the water to reach excessively high summer temperatures. When the temperature exceeds their comfort level, crappie get lethargic and tough to catch. There's one place, however, where crappie still find comfort—inside hollow cypress trees.

Crappie often hide in the confines of a dark cypress hollow.

The best trees have small to medium openings to the interior, thus excluding most outside light. Don't drop a minnow or jig inside the tree, but dangle it enticingly just outside the opening. Crappie will dart out when they see your offering, then usually rush back inside. Use heavy line, set the hook quickly and try to keep the fish outside the hollow so it doesn't tangle you.

Fish Storm Fronts

Summer weather tends to be stable, with minimal effects on crappie activity. But when conditions are such that afternoon thunderstorms are popping up day after day, plan an outing that allows you to fish just before a storm hits. Don't be on the water during periods of lightning or high wind. But if you can do it safely, be fishing when the clouds start to thicken and the wind picks up. Just before a storm hits, crappie often move to surface strata and feed actively. The action may last only a few minutes, but during those few minutes, you may catch more fish than you will the rest of the day.

Side-trolling

When trolling for summer crappie, try mounting your trolling motor on the side of the boat instead of the front. This allows you to move in a very slow, controlled fashion so you can mine deep structures more efficiently.

Pumping Iron

Summer crappie often suspend in 10 to 20 feet of water around the branches of standing submerged trees. To reach them quickly, lower a small jigging spoon on a tight line directly down through the branches. Give the spoon a short upward pull at every three feet of depth. Crappie often inhale the lure as it falls, and you won't know one is on unless you raise your rod tip.

After the Storm

When a summer storm ends, look for crappie in the thickest available cover—buckbrush, willow thickets, etc. Allow the wind to blow your boat against the cover. Use a long pole to work a jig into the brush, then fish little pockets most folks miss. Fish the jig with little movement, and work each hole.

Weed Them Out

Green aquatic vegetation attracts baitfish in summer with the offer of protection, shade and abundant oxygen. Crappie follow. Summer crappie anglers should, too.

Fish weedbeds using a $1/64$- to $1/16$-ounce jig placed one to four feet below a small bobber, casting into open pockets or working the lure along one edge. Retrieve in jerk-stop fashion, pulling with a hard tug so the jig rises toward the surface, then stopping long enough to allow the jig to sink perpendicular to the surface again.

Care for Your Catch

Summer crappie placed in a stale livewell or on a stringer in hot surface water soon die and become soggy. For good-eating fish, take along an ice chest containing several inches of cracked ice. Cover the ice with a wet towel before dropping in your catch, and drain the melted ice frequently to prevent your fish from sitting in water. The result is firm, fresh fillets that have the delicate, delicious flavor for which crappie are famous.

In water discolored by turnover, crappie usually hold tight to cover and structure, so anglers should present baits and lures tight to cover as well.

FALL: Understanding Fall Transition

The summer-to-autumn transition period is a frustrating time for many. One day, crappie are deep; the next, they're on top. Where fish nailed anything yesterday, they refuse everything today. As the seasons are changing, so are the daily routines.

You'll often hear this referred to as the "fall turnover" season because the water is "turning over" as the cooling surface layer sinks and warmer bottom water is pushed upward. Some anglers write this off as a terrible time to fish. But turnover needn't be the nemesis many perceive it to be. Crappie fans can actually benefit from this fall phenomenon, if they understand it.

Fall Turnover

During summer, many lakes stratify into three distinct layers. These lakes have a layer of cold, poorly oxygenated water on bottom, and a layer of warm, moderately oxygenated water on top. Because cold water is heavier than warm water (to a certain degree), warmer water stays on top and colder water sinks to the bottom. In between lies a layer of cool, oxygen-rich water called the thermocline. Summer crappie are usually found in or near the thermocline because that layer best satisfies their needs for oxygen and water temperature.

In late summer, fall or early winter (the exact time depends largely on the latitude where the lake is found), cool weather begins lowering the surface water temperature. As the upper layer cools, it becomes heavier and sinks. This action forces the warmer, lighter water below back to the surface. This water is subsequently cooled, just as the previous surface layer was, and descends as it cools. This mixing or "turnover" continues for several weeks until the thermocline disappears and all water in the lake is roughly the same temperature. This mixing effect also replenishes oxygen in deep water.

The end result is that fish formerly restricted to narrow bands of acceptable oxygen and temperature levels are no longer limited in their movements. Crappie once barred from the coolest depths because of low oxygen levels may now roam freely to much deeper water. Likewise, where once fish could not spend extended periods in extreme shallows due to high temperatures and low oxygen levels, after turnover even these areas are acceptable. Crappie now may be found deep, shallow or anywhere in between.

Technically, turnover continues until the surface water temperature drops below 39 degrees. Water is heaviest at this temperature and sinks to the bottom. Cooler water "floats" on top. This is why our lakes freeze from the top down, rather than from the bottom up. And this represents the annual end of the turnover process.

Lake Turnover Signs

The time of year when turnover occurs varies by latitude. Fishermen in cooler areas may begin turnover strategies in September; warmer regions may not have turnover until January.

On many lakes, turnover is clearly visible. A change in water color is evident as circulating water brings up bottom debris.

The water may take on a milky or brownish tint and smell like rotten eggs or decaying vegetation.

Turnover in some lakes is invisible and therefore confusing even to those familiar with the phenomenon. In these waters, the only indication turnover is occurring may be distinct changes in crappie behavior after a few weeks of cool weather. For instance, crappie caught on deep humps one week may be ambushing baitfish near shorelines the next.

Some waters don't experience turnover because they don't stratify in summer. Rivers are a case in point. So are many large, shallow, windswept lakes and some reservoirs with lock-and-dam facilities or hydroelectric generators. In extreme southern areas, south Florida for example, temperatures may not drop low enough for turnover to occur.

Turnover Fishing Problems

The biggest problem most anglers face is pinpointing fish. In summer, most crappie were in or near the thermocline. Shallow-water action might be good during cool, low-light periods, but you could be certain no crappie would be caught in the "dead zone" below the thermocline.

Fall turnover drastically changes all this. With acceptable levels of oxygen from top to bottom, and no discernible temperature change from the shallowest shallows to the deepest depths, crappie can be almost anywhere.

Dealing with Turnover Fishing Problems

The secret to turnover success is realizing that crappie still concentrate in areas providing the most comfortable living conditions and then learning to identify those areas. Theoretically, conditions are now such that crappie can live anywhere within the lake. Actually, factors such as oxygen content, light penetration and food availability still greatly influence a crappie's choice of living quarters.

Consider, for instance, that all the debris and poorly oxygenated water being pushed upwards from the lake bed when turnover begins temporarily "trashes" the whole system. Crappie respond by seeking areas with good quality water. To find them, anglers do likewise. An easy way is to work tributaries bringing fresh water into the lake. Another way is to look for areas where turnover has not begun. On some large lakes, different arms of the lake turn over at different times, and anglers can concentrate their efforts in areas that aren't visibly affected.

When turnover causes excessive amounts of decaying debris to circulate in the water column, sudden significant drops in oxygen can result. When this happens, crappie must find oxygenated water immediately. They frequently solve the problem by going directly to the nearest source, which is surface aeration from wind and waves. Consequently, windswept shorelines in fairly shallow cover may be productive crappie fishing spots.

During the final few weeks of turnover, as the water starts to clear, crappie often concentrate on vertical structure. This is some bottom feature offering great depth variance with little or no horizontal movement necessary. Good examples are bluff banks, bridge pilings and fast-dropping slopes along creek and river channels. In such places, crappie can alter their depth according to prevailing light penetration and other factors by merely moving up or down the structures as conditions dictate.

Brushy treetops and standing timber also attract crappie during this part of turnover. When weed beds begin dying and decaying in late fall, crappie often migrate to open lake areas where inundated trees line underwater creek and river channels. Here the fish can move shallow or deep as water and weather conditions dictate. On cloudy or windy days when light won't penetrate very far into the water, crappie may be within a foot or two of the surface. Bright, sunny, post-frontal days may find them hugging the bottom.

In autumn, water conditions are such that crappie may now be found deep, shallow or anywhere in between. Pinpointing fish often is tough, but persistence pays dividends when crappie are found.

Crappie and Vertical Structure

Because crappie orienting to vertical structure can be anywhere between the bottom and the surface, pinpointing them may require extra effort. Begin by thoroughly fishing different depths until fish are located. If the water is still discolored, light penetration will be restricted, and crappie will move shallower. Thus, the angler should begin by fishing shallow reaches first. As the water clears, however, bright sunlight will drive most crappie into the depths or under heavy cover. In this situation, fish first around deeper hideouts.

The key is to efficiently check all depths until a crappie is caught. Then work that depth thoroughly for additional fish. When you've established the level where fish are holding, then move to other vertical structures and work the same depth. Chances are good you'll encounter another school of crappie at some point along the way.

Fall crappie often hold near steep vertical structures such as rock ledges that allow quick movement from shallow to deep water and vice versa.

Fishing Other Types of Structure and Cover

The places you can find fall crappie action are almost innumerable. Long, sloping points are always a good possibility, as are humps and inundated islands. Crappie like old fencerows running from shallow to deep water, and large trees that have toppled into fairly deep water near the shoreline should definitely be investigated. Other favorite areas include Christmas tree fish attractors, timbered areas edging underwater ditches and ponds, submerged rockpiles, stump fields, and saddle areas between islands.

Best Lures for Fall Turnover

As always, lure selection depends primarily on water and weather conditions, available forage and the physical characteristics of the area you're fishing. But remembering these tips should help you make the best selection.
   1. If visibility is severely restricted due to circulating debris, crappie will rely more on sound, vibrations and odor to find food. Using lures with rattles, flashy spin-

ners, spray-on scents and other attention-getters may improve success.
2. Because crappie in stained water stay closer to the structure they're using, work baits and lures closer than usual to cover in dingy water. Bumping the cover may be necessary to elicit strikes.
3. As turnover waters clear, crappie move deeper. That's when it's time to use tiny lures fished on light line. Small jigs, spoons and lipless crankbaits are among the best.
4. During turnover, shad schools chased by feeding crappie may pop to the surface anywhere at any time. Keep an ultralight rod-and-reel combo handy that has a silver jig, small spoon or other shad-like lure tied on.
5. Don't depend only on lures. A shiner minnow rigged to remain lively is one of the best of all crappie attractors during turnover. Savvy anglers carry a variety of lures and a good supply of minnows when fishing this time of year. If one thing doesn't work, another probably will if you can figure out what it is. Work each area thoroughly, but if you don't have a strike after 15 minutes or so, rig with something different.

River Fishing During Fall Turnover

Because rivers are relatively unaffected by turnover, they provide an excellent alternative for anglers dealing with "turnover turmoil." In summer, high temperatures drive river crappie to deep-water haunts, usually in or near the main river channel. Autumn offers more moderate water temperatures, allowing

Pro Tip

"When fishing standing timber, fish each tree for only a couple of seconds. If you don't get a bite, move to the next tree. It is easy to catch the active crappie. Too many people make the mistake of sitting or tying up to a tree. You will catch more fish by using your trolling motor and moving from tree to tree."

--Kevin Rogers,
Crappie USA Classic qualifier six consecutive years

crappie to reinvade shallow, off-channel areas where they were found during the spring spawn. They're often in backwaters, river-connected oxbows and other areas where current is inappreciable. Because the water in these areas is shallower, crappie are easier to find, too. And they're more aggressive than they were in summer—hungry and eager to bite.

During the late weeks of summer and early weeks of fall, look for river crappie near wing dikes, logjams, willow thickets and other current-breaking structure in or near the main body of the river. As temperatures drop and autumn gets in full swing, look for them near willows, cypress trees and other woody cover off the main river in oxbows and backwaters. As autumn turns to winter, look for crappie moving back to deep-water haunts near the main river channel.

In Conclusion

The transition from summer to autumn is jolting for both fish and fishermen. Crappie find their once secure world literally turned over on them. Crappie anglers find their quarry more unpredictable than ever. Overcoming this seasonal nemesis will require all the skill, knowledge and patience you can muster. But when you finally zero in on a big school of hefty autumn crappie, you're sure to agree that the rewards make the extra effort worthwhile.

Bankfishing Options

If you enjoy crappie fishing and usually fish from the bank, don't miss the action in autumn. Fall crappie often move to shallow cover-infested haunts and are easily taken using a long pole to work jigs or minnows in brushy shoreline cover.

Public fishing piers are often productive during this season. Brush piles or other man-made fish attractors placed around them, frequently draw schools of big slabs. Use an ultralight spinning combo, using a $1^{1}/_{16}$-ounce jig, cast around to determine the location of the attractor. Then cast to or beside the attractor and count the jig down until you get a strike or hit brush. If you get a strike, use the same count next cast. If you hit brush, use a shorter count. Learn to establish positive depth control and you'll soon be putting crappie on your stringer.

Jigs with bright bream-like colors may outperform others in fall.

Fall Fishing Tips

Autumn is a golden season for crappie fishing fans. Summer's crowds have finally vanished. Lakes, ponds and rivers shimmer beneath canopies of vermilion and amber leaves. Summer-fattened crappie are in prime condition, offering exciting possibilities for action-hungry anglers.

This golden season offers some of the year's finest crappie angling, and if you simply take the time you can easily learn some handy tips that will help you locate and tempt these silvery panfish. Read on, and you will.

Trolling Jigs

Try trolling with jigs to find often-scattered schools of autumn crappie. This tactic works best if you periodically change your trolling speed and the size of jig you use. Start with a 1/32-ounce jig and a fast trolling speed. This will find crappie in shallow water. If that doesn't work, try a 1/16-ounce jig and a medium trolling speed to look for crappie in mid-depths. If necessary, change again, to a ⅛-ounce jig and a medium-slow speed, then a ⅛-ounce jig and a very slow speed.

Back Out With the Fish

When fishing a reservoir that has current caused by power generation, it pays to observe changes in the amount of current. Crappie may be in as little as four to five feet of water when current is minimal, but when power generation increases and current is high, crappie will move out to structures 10 to 20 feet deep. In the latter situation, work offshore cover, positioning your boat directly above and dropping minnows straight down. Or back off and cast ⅛-ounce jigs dressed with curly-tailed grubs or tubes.

Get to the Point

If the water level starts dropping fast due to power generation, try fishing points using small in-line or safety-pin spinners. Retrieve the lure with an up-and-down "yo-yo" motion, or buzz it along the surface and allow it to fall or "die" right beside the cover. Position your boat in deep water and cast toward the shallow part of the point, or vice versa.

Shallow Water Wading

Crappie often move to extreme shallows, water barely deep enough to cover them, as the water temperature cools. You may catch more if you don a set of waders and carefully make your way to edge areas fringed with inundated brush, willows or grass. Use a 12- to 14-foot jigging pole, pull the jig to the tip, then after positioning the jig over a hole in the cover, lower the jig into the crappie hideout.

Sliders for Stumps

Stump fields in mid-depths are prime holding areas for fall crappie, but stumps often gobble up so many tube jigs that you spend more time tying than fishing. In this situation, try a slider jig such as Blakemore's Road Runner Jaker Jig or Charlie Brewer's Weedless Crappie Slider. Cast past the stumps, let the lure settle, then retrieve the lure slow and steady. If you hit wood before catching a crappie, continue your retrieve, allowing the jig to bump over the wood. Most times, you'll be able to work the lure in this fashion without hangups.

Use Some Scents

When an autumn cold front passes, you may entice persnickety crappie to bite by spraying your lure or bait with a liquid or gel scents. Not all these scents work, but if you test several brands on a regular basis, you'll find that some will definitely enhance the number of strikes you get when crappie are finicky. The crappie will hold on better, too, increasing your chance of getting a good hookset.

Fish Windward Shores

Wind can be an important factor in determining where you're most likely to find early fall crappie. Wind pushes tiny invertebrates that minnows and other baitfish eat. If there's a westerly wind for a couple of days, an east-shore area could hold the most fish, or vice versa. Consequently, you should always give wind-hit areas your full attention.

Rock and Roll

During late fall, as aquatic vegetation dies, crappie often move to deep rock piles in waters where such structures are found. The best rock piles are associated with humps, outside channel bends, saddles between rises and other prominent bottom structure. Fish them with a rig made by tying a ⅜- to ½-ounce bell sinker at your line's end. Place a snelled hook 12 inches above the sinker on a dropper loop, then tie a ¹⁄₁₆-ounce jig directly to your line 18 inches above the hook. Bait the hook with a lively minnow, then drag the rig across the bottom near the rock pile until you catch a crappie. When you find your quarry, position your boat right over the strike zone and switch to a vertical presentation, which will help you avoid spooking other crappie.

Cedars and Shad

Not all crappie hold on deep structures in late fall. Often crappie follow schools of shad into the backs of feeder creeks, holding in four to six feet of water along the edges of channel breaks. If you can find cedar brush piles or tops in such areas, chances are you've found a mother lode of crappie. Work the tops with a stationary slip-float and minnow rig, or use a vertical jigging tightline tactic with jigs.

Return for Wayward Suspenders

At times, your fish finder may pinpoint a bit of key structure—an isolated stump, for example, or a rock pile—that is void of crappie. When you find such areas, slowly circle around that spot and look for suspended fish. If you find them, make note of the structure's location, then return to it later. You might find that these previously inactive crappie have moved onto the structure and begun feeding.

"See" Edges that are Out of Sight

Fall crappie often hold along creek channel drop-offs and other edge areas. You'll be able to fish such a location better if you mark it with a several buoys. Locate the drop-off with sonar, then slowly follow the edge. Throw out a marker buoy each time you cross a certain depth—10 feet, for instance. Continue placing the buoys, about 20 feet apart, until you've used them all. Now you have a visible image of the edge and can fish it more thoroughly for crappie.

Try Bream-Like Lures

In ponds and small lakes, crappie often stay fat and healthy by eating a diet heavy on juvenile sunfish. In these waters, particularly those with clear water, your fall catch rate may soar if you fish with lures resembling tiny bream in color and/or shape. Jigs with some combination of red, gold and green colors work especially well in this situation, as do small sunfish-imitation crankbaits and spinners with gold blades and brightly colored bodies.

Soft-Plastic Minnows

Crappie anglers often overlook another class of lures that are dynamite on fall slabs. Realistic soft-plastic baitfish such as the Banjo Glitter Minnow and Snag Proof's Moss Master Swimmin' Shad not only come in a variety of sizes and colors, but they're weedless as well, allowing you to place them right in the middle of thick cover where crappie are likely to be.

Catching slow-biting winter crappie can be tough at times, but anglers who know tips for success will probably learn that cold-water fishing isn't as difficult as they imagined.

WINTER: Ice-Box Slabs

Catching winter crappie can be challenging. If the water temperature falls extremely low, crappie may become lethargic and bite so gingerly they are almost undetectable. Nevertheless, crappie are commonly caught by ice fishermen, and other anglers. With tips for success you will discover that winter fishing isn't as difficult as you thought it would be.

When fishing deep-water crappie haunts, nothing can beat an ultralight rod and a tiny reel filled with 2- or 4-pound test line. This rig exhibits sensitivity not found with larger tackle and permits you to detect the most delicate nibbles. It also turns every fish you hook into a whopper. Fighting a big crappie up out of 25 feet of water on 2 pound line and a mere switch of a rod isn't as easy as it sounds.

If crappie are suspended, try fishing a jig or minnow under a bobber. If they aren't deeper than the length of your rod or pole, you can merely put a bobber on your line and dangle the lure or bait below it at the proper depth. When you cast, the bait sinks to the right depth and stays there while you retrieve it with twitches that lend a lifelike action.

Chances are, however, you'll find crappie much deeper this season than your rod is long, up to 25 or 30 feet in some cases. When this is the case, rig a sliding bobber above the jig or minnow to make casting easier. To do this, place a bobber stop on your line at the depth you want to fish. Then add a bead below the stop, followed by the sliding bobber. Finish the rig by adding a split shot and hook for minnow fishing or by tying on the jig.

When the bobber hits the water, the weight of the jig or bait rig pulls line through the bobber until the bobber stop abuts the float. Your bait is automatically at the depth you selected, and you can easily adjust the depth by moving the bobber stop up or down the line. The stop will easily pass through your line guides and winds onto the reel spool. It's simple and effective.

A jig/live minnow combination is a popular winter crappie enticement. The jig hook is run upward through the minnow's lips, and the rig is trolled or cast. Because crappie in cold water often bite short, some anglers add a stinger hook, a short length

Pro Tip

"When fishing in the winter or in cold water conditions, always have a pole in your hand with a few fingertips on the line. The bite is very light this time of year. If you aren't holding the pole, you will never feel or see the bite."
--Richard Williams, Kentucky Lake crappie guide

of line tied to the bend of the jig hook on one end and to a small treble hook on the other end. The minnow is lip-hooked on the jig, then one barb of the treble is hooked in the minnow's tail. This rigging is somewhat troublesome, but stingers help nail soft-hitting crappie that would otherwise be missed.

One of my favorite lures for winter crappie is the Blakeley Road Runner. This horsehead spinner can be cast and retrieved up and down points, over and around humps and along deep sand bars and flats. It has what I call a double whammy—the flash of a spinner and the seductive dance of a marabou or rubber-skirted jig all wrapped up in one deadly little package. Use a varied retrieve, sometimes fast, sometimes slow, sometimes smooth, sometimes jerky. Occasionally, let the lure fall to the bottom then rip it upward again. All these shenanigans usually will be more than crappie can bear, and the flash of the little spinner whirling through the water just ahead of the action tail entices strikes from even the most finicky fish.

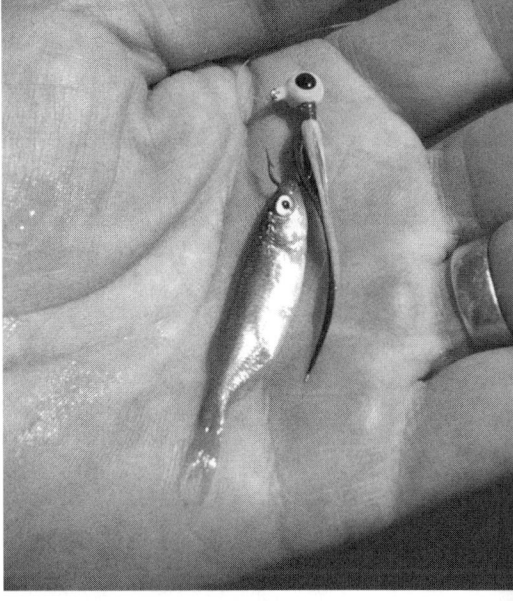

The jig/minnow combination—a marriage of crappie fishing's two most popular enticements—is one of the best of all winter crappie-catchers.

Yet another method of taking crappie on deep winter structure is to slow-troll with tandem-rigged jigs. Trolling covers a lot of water and will often produce fish on those days when crappie don't want to cooperate. Trolling with jigs set at different depths also is one of the best methods for taking suspended crappie holding at mid-depths. Suspended fish often are hard to catch by casting or jigging.

When you're trolling at these greater depths and the fish are not responding, try pumping the rod with a long sweeping action. The lures crawl along, then hop a few feet above the bottom and fall back. This constant series of swimming, diving and jigging action incites crappie to strike.

If an electrical power plant is adjacent to the body of water you're fishing, be sure to look for crappie nearby. These facilities are hotspots in the literal sense of the term. Lake or river water is used to cool internal machinery, and when the water is returned from whence it came, it's usually much warmer than the surrounding lake or stream. Shad and other baitfish congregate in these warm environs like bathers on a Caribbean beach, and crappie move in to gluttonize the schools. Warmer water raises the metabolic rate of cold-blooded slabs, meaning more frequent, active feeding periods during winter. Savvy anglers take advantage of this unique situation.

Try a 1/16- or 1/8-ounce jig (depending on the amount of current). Cast it across or up the current and retrieve it at different depths. Start by letting the lure sink three or four feet, and if this doesn't work, go deeper and deeper until you're working it just over the bottom.

As winter draws to a close, water temperature climbs toward the mid-50s, and crappie begin moving to staging areas that provide quick access between winter's deep haunts and spring's shallow spawning zones. Tributaries bringing warmer water into a lake can be crappie hotspots at this time. Other good structures include inundated creek or river channels, long sloping points and drop-offs along shallow flats.

The same lures and tackle used earlier will work when fishing these staging areas, but faster presentations may be possible. As the water warms from the upper 40s through the low 50s toward the ideal spawning temperature of 56 degrees, crappie become more aggressive.

Winter fishing isn't for everybody. For most of us, a warm fireplace is much more attractive than a frigid outing on a cold lake.

If the fishing itch gets too intense to bear, though, give winter crappie a try; a sure remedy for what ails you.

DID YOU KNOW?

Winter is a great time to target crappie. During this season, crappie bunch up in large schools and suspend over deep water and creek ledges. White crappie tend to gang up in creeks, and black crappie bunch up in deep water targeting threadfin shad. Crappie will be around big schools of shad, so if your electronics is showing large schools of shad, you know crappie are right below ready to ambush the baitfish. Anglers can rig up with live bait or jigs. Crappie will hit both in deep water in winter.

Fishing underwater fish attractors made from old Christmas trees and other materials is a sure-fire way to zero in on schools of winter crappie.

Christmas Tree Crappie

Winter crappie usually hold on deep cover and structure, making them somewhat difficult to locate. In recent years, though, fisheries managers have sought to bring crappie and anglers together by placing man-made fish attractors in many first-rate crappie lakes.

These artificial crappie "condos" are usually made from trees bundled together with wire and sunk with concrete weights. They're especially helpful to anglers unfamiliar with a lake's bottom topography and to those who don't have sophisticated electronic equipment for locating crappie concentrations on underwater structure. Because fish attractors placed by government agencies are usually marked with specially colored buoys, all the angler must do to find crappie is move from one fish-attractor buoy to another, working jigs and minnows through the woody tangles below.

How Man-Made Fish Attractors Work

Fishermen have been sinking brush and trees to attract and concentrate fish for hundreds of years. Sink a tree in a lake where much of the natural cover has disappeared, and crappie will flock to it like a new restaurant in town. These sites provide crappie a place to rest and feed and also provide potential spawning habitat.

Old Christmas trees are among the most often used materials for making crappie attractors. These are usually gathered at advertised collection sites, tied in bundles and anchored with concrete blocks to supplement existing cover. Within a few days after the trees are sunk, small aquatic organisms gather around the maze of branches and twigs. When baitfish discover these minute food animals, they begin schooling around the brush piles to feed on them. Crappie soon follow, feeding on the schools of baitfish. Then fishermen can zero in on the concentrations of crappie.

Christmas trees aren't the only material used for building crappie attractors. One variation uses several small hardwood trees bundled together with wire. Wooden stake beds also work well. Long, thin slats of lumber are driven into the lake bed or nailed to shipping pallets for sinking in deeper water. Many state agencies use bundles of old tires with holes punched in them to facilitate sinking. Concrete blocks attached with wire hold the attractors on the bottom.

The Barkley Lake Brush Pile Study

A 1978 study on Lake Barkley, a 57,920-acre reservoir in Kentucky and Tennessee, proved that Christmas-tree fish shelters attract more and larger crappie than areas without such structures. The study showed that each acre of brush averaged 1,530 crappie, while an acre without brush contained only 319 crappies. In areas with brush, crappie were 10 times larger in average weight than areas without brush piles.

Based on this data, the Kentucky Department of Fish and Wildlife Resources, the Tennessee Wildlife Resources Agency

and the Tennessee Valley Authority began placing brush pile fish attractors in several Tennessee Valley reservoirs, including Barkley and Kentucky lakes. Tens of thousands of individual structures were placed in dozens of lakes.

Over the years since they were first placed in these lakes, fish attractors have helped heighten Kentucky and Barkley lakes' reputations as two of the country's finest crappie fisheries. Using maps that are available to help pinpoint brush piles, even first-time visitors can cash in on the bonanza of blue-ribbon crappie fishing served up by these enormous impoundments.

Fishing sunken brushpiles is easier if you first delineate the boundaries of each fish attractor using marker buoys.

The Bull Shoals/Norfork Fish Cover Project

A more recent large-scale fish-attractor project took place in lakes Bull Shoals and Norfork, two large U.S. Army Corps of Engineers impoundments on the Arkansas-Missouri state line.

The Corps completed construction of Norfork Lake in 1944 and Bull Shoals Lake in 1952. The main purpose of these reservoirs was to provide flood control and hydropower. During construction, virtually all trees were removed from what would later be the lakes' bottoms. The trees that were not removed have mostly rotted away and only trunks remain.

Because the lake levels fluctuate dramatically, aquatic vegetation has never become well-established in Norfork and Bull Shoals. Lack of fish cover has always been a limiting factor in fish production in the lakes.

Still, crappie and other fish grow very fast in the clear, high-quality water, and fishing is excellent for those who know where to find their quarry. Unfortunately, lack of cover made it difficult for many anglers to locate concentrations of sportfish.

In 1986, the Twin Lakes Chapter of the Bass Research Foundation approached the Arkansas Game & Fish Commission with a special request. They wanted assistance introducing aquatic vegetation into Norfork and Bull Shoals to improve fish habitat and fishing. At the time, the Corps and the Commission were concerned that establishing aquatic vegetation might conflict with other reservoir uses. The Game & Fish Commission suggested that a large-scale artificial habitat improvement project might accomplish some of the same goals.

A plan involving use of trees from the lakes' shorelines to create fish attractors was presented to the Corps and the U.S. Fish Wildlife Service for federal funding approval through the Sportfish Restoration Act. Both federal agencies and the Twin Lakes Chapter of Bass Research Foundation approved the plan, and the project began in earnest in 1987.

Anglers young and old can quickly learn successful methods for catching crappie on man-made fish attractors.

Since the project began, 600 fish attractors have been installed in Bull Shoals and Norfork. Over 70,000 trees comprise the attractors, which cover over 160 acres of lake bottom totaling 33 miles in length.

Each attractor is composed of 30 or more bundles of trees (six or less trees per bundle, depending on size) and covers an area approximately 40 feet wide and 300 feet long. The bundles were sunk along a contour line that corresponds to the depth at which the thermocline usually forms (25 feet deep). On Bull Shoals, the target elevation is 630 feet above mean sea level (msl), and on Norfork, it's 525 feet above msl. Fishermen can figure out how deep the attractors are by calling a Corps lake information line, getting the current lake levels and subtracting the above elevations.

Fish attractors have been placed in many other Arkansas lakes as well. These include outstanding crappie waters such as Bob Kidd, Elmdale, Chicot, Dierks, DeQueen, Sugarloaf, Hinkle and several lakes on Dagmar Wildlife Management Area.

In other states, fish attractors now are common features in many first-rate crappie lakes as well. All such lakes offer excellent late-winter crappie angling for those who know how to fish sunken brush piles.

Fishing Brush Piles

Bill Fletcher of Mountain Home, Arkansas, has guided fishermen on Lake Norfork for decades. He's done an extensive fish-attractor program on his own for his guide service and was instrumental in

"If you set your own crappie structure in a lake, consider using five-gallon plastic buckets. Fill them about three-fourths full of gravel and set them in the lake. The plastic will never rot. Within a month, the fish can't tell the difference between a bucket or a stump. I usually throw a marker out and put 10 to 12 buckets around the marker. I have done this in several places on Kentucky Lake and made stump fields. The buckets are cheap, they're easy to put out, and they work."

--Richard Williams, Kentucky Lake crappie guide

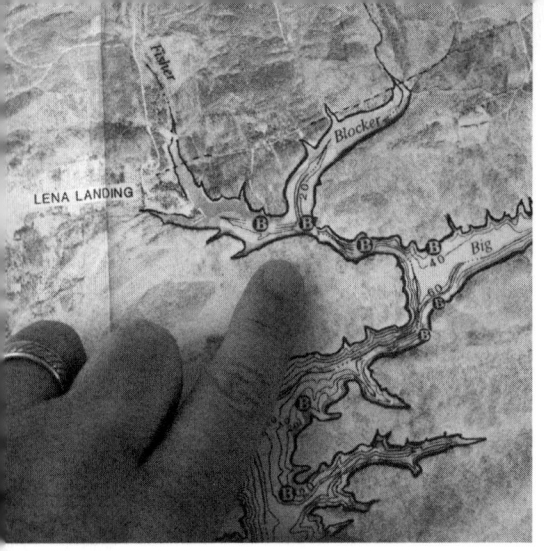

Bait and tackle shops often carry lake maps that show the locations of permanent brushpiles and other fish attractors.

the completion of the Lake Norfork fish cover project.

"Lake Norfork was over 90 percent cleared when it was built," he says. "Now the brush piles placed in the lake are magnets for crappie and other species like bass and walleyes.

"These brush piles can make a big difference for crappie fishermen," Fletcher continues, "especially someone fishing a big deep lake like Norfork for the first time. One of the biggest helps for me as a guide is, I can take someone out who's never fished here before, and on a half-a-day trip, I can show them how to locate brush piles with a graph and how to fish them. Then they can come back to the lake and have a successful fishing trip on their own."

After choosing a fish-attractor site marked with a buoy, Fletcher runs his boat over the site, using a graph recorder to determine the positioning of the brush.

"On Norfork and Bull Shoals, the brush piles will extend about 100 to 150 feet on each side of the buoy, and about 90 percent of them will be centered on the 20-25 foot depth," Fletcher notes. "Begin by using your graph to find the shallowest brush pile, and mark it with a buoy. Crappie that are in an

Recycle Christmas Trees

You can build your own crappie attractors by recycling Christmas trees after the holiday season. Attach a concrete block to the base of each tree to anchor it. If placed in deep enough water, the trees will stand upright, and due to the upwards sweep of the branches, your hook won't be easily snagged when you work jigs or minnows around them.

For most anglers, a few properly placed fish attractors are adequate. Place some deep, some shallow, some on flats, some on ledges and stream channels, and you'll always have a productive crappie spot regardless of the time of year. Plot the locations of the attractors in a GPS or triangulate using three landmarks to guide you to the exact spot. When you are in the immediate area of the cover, you can spot it with sonar or fan-cast jigs to locate it.

Some government agencies such as the U.S. Army Corps of Engineers have restrictions on placing crappie cover in lakes under their jurisdiction. Check for such restrictions before placing your cover in any public water.

aggressive or 'biting' posture will often be lined up horizontally above the shallowest brush piles, so fish these piles first."

Fletcher recommends a count-down technique for pinpointing feeding fish.

"Take your boat a cast away from your marker buoy, 20 or 30 feet, and using 4-pound test line and a 1/16-ounce jig head, cast to the buoy," he says. "Now count the jig down until you get a hit or hit brush. If you get a hit, use the same count next cast. If you hit brush, use a shorter count.

"The key to catching crappie on fish attractors is positive depth control," Fletcher continues. Crappie don't feed down, they bite up. So don't fish under them. Sometimes crappie will form horizontal schools on the sides of the brush piles, but the same tactics will work if you can locate them.

"You can catch crappie without the brush piles," says Fletcher, "but brush piles certainly make it easier. You establish that the fish are there and at a certain depth, then boom, boom, boom, you're putting them in the boat."

Now, the old excuse, "Winter crappie are too hard to find," just doesn't hold water. With a map and sonar, any crappie angler can easily find man-made fish attractors holding plenty of big slabs. Where fish shelters are marked with buoys, it's even easier.

Don't wait for spring to enjoy the thrill of crappie fishing. Bundle up, and indulge in some first-rate fishing fun. Christmas-tree crappie provide a sure cure for winter's cabin blues.

Tips for Fishing Crappie Attractors

- Slowly ease your anchor to the bottom on either side of the attractor.
- Lower the bait or lure until you feel brush; note the depth until you are within the crappie's strike zone. Fish minnows below a bobber. Move jigs or small spoons slowly up and down in and around the brush.
- Cast small crankbaits, spinners and jig/spinner combos from a boat anchored off to one side of the attractor. Work the lure over the top of the brush pile or along the sides.
- Using thin wire hooks that bend easily helps lessen the need for re-rigging due to hangups.

The Heddon Sonar and other bladebaits are superb winter crappie lures.

Winter Fishing Tips

Fishing for winter crappie can be beautifully simple. Yet many crappie anglers take this simplicity a step too far. One or two proven tactics and baits command most of their fishing time, and if these don't produce ... well, there's always next time.

You can greatly improve your winter crappie-fishing success by trying a few new concepts and techniques. Stick to traditional approaches when they're producing slabs. But when "regular" tactics don't work, the following tricks can make your catch rate soar.

Slayed With a Blade

Among the many overlooked winter crappie enticements are blade-baits. Perennial favorites include ¼- and ⅜-ounce Heddon Sonars, Cordell Gay Blades and Reef Runner Cicadas. These compact lures sink quickly and maintain depth when worked yo-yo fashion around deep structure and cover.

An upward rod sweep lifts the bait, causing a fish-attracting vibration. As the rod is lowered, the lure begins a spiral fall that triggers an instinctive attack from crappie.

To eliminate line twist, snip the line eight inches above the lure and tie a barrel swivel to both cut ends.

Winter Springs

Underwater springs bubbling up in the bottom of a lake often attract concentrations of winter crappie. Spring water stays at a constant temperature year-round, usually between 60 and 70 degrees, thus providing a place where crappie warm up in winter. Temperature gauges can help locate springs, or use an outdoor thermometer tied to a string to detect changes in water temperature. Watch, too, for springs that reveal their presence by altering the surface of the water slightly. The water around a spring is usually clearer than the rest of a lake, so use lighter line and smaller, realistic lures or live minnows.

The winter crappie angler can use many proven tactics to catch a mess of crappie in cold water.

Trap Your Quarry

Vertical jigging with a tiny lipless crankbait such as the Bill Lewis Tiny Trap, Cordell's Super Spot or Mann's Finn Mann is deadly on winter crappie suspended around structure such as sunken islands, rock ridges and logs. Position your boat over the target structure, then lower the lure to the bottom. Engage your reel and take up slack. Jerk the lure off the bottom two to three feet, and let it free-fall. Maneuver your boat along structure, jigging the lure this way.

Chapter V: Crappie Seasons

Pier Pressure

Winter bank fishing can be unproductive because crappie move to offshore cover. But when nasty weather keeps you shorebound, try fishing at the end of a public fishing pier. When such a structure is built, a deeper hole usually is created near the outside end, and frequently, brush piles are added to attract crappie.

Farm Fishing

Farm ponds also provide possibilities for shore anglers. First, be sure the pond contains crappie; many don't. If it does, and the owner grants permission to fish, you're in business. Head to the levee that impounds the water. Big slabs frequently are taken by casting to woody cover here. My favorite lure in this situation is a large safety-pin spinner, but carry of a variety of lures, and keep changing until you determine what is most productive.

Be a Weather Watcher

The best winter crappie fishing often comes toward the end of a fairly long warm spell as winter draws to a close. To pick the best days, watch the weather report. If the meteorologist says a cold front is approaching after several warm days, plan some fishing time. With luck, you'll find male crappie starting to fan their beds in shallows, and females looking for food nearby. Therefore, focus fishing efforts on shallow waters where spawning will occur. A minnow worked shallow under a bobber is the ticket here.

Look for Ledges

When using sonar, scan for shallow underwater ledges—ditches, cuts and gullies—near bankside bluffs or coves. Ledges are especially productive when found near timber, brush piles or other crappie cover.

One-sixteenth to ⅛-ounce jigs are ideal lures for fishing ledges. Work a jig down the drop-off, hopping it in stairstep fashion until you get a hit.

Use a GPS

GPS units are more affordable than ever, with some priced less than $100. These high-tech marvels translate satellite signals into data an angler can navigate by to return to first-rate winter fishing areas such as brush piles and open-water drop-offs.

Don't waste time triangulating with landmarks or watching a depthfinder to find your favorite winter fishing holes. Learn to use a GPS and you can be fishing instead of looking.

Head for the Headwaters

Headwaters areas tend to produce the best winter fishing. The headwaters area is the upper end, usually opposite the dam, where the major stream or streams feeding the lake flow into it. Late-winter crappie become active earlier in headwaters because this is where the water first begins to warm. Creeks and small streams above the lake warm first because they are shallow and fed by the first warming rains. These in turn feed larger streams flowing into the lake, and they, too, warm up before the deeper main lake.

Remember this when planning a fishing trip this time of year. Headwaters usually outproduce other portions of a lake.

Soft Strikes

When a winter crappie strikes, it usually feels "soft", like the bait has picked up a leaf or little stick. Be prepared to set the hook the instant your line goes slack or your bait doesn't feel right. Learn to be a line watcher. Using fluorescent line and wearing polarized sunglasses improves your ability to detect subtle strikes.

"Winter is my favorite time to target crappie. During this season, crappie bunch up in large schools and suspend over deep water and creek ledges. White crappie tend to gang up in creeks, and black crappie bunch up in deep water targeting threadfin shad. Crappie will be around big schools of shad, so if your electronics is showing large schools of shad, you know crappie are right below ready to ambush the baitfish. Anglers can rig up with live bait or jigs. Crappie will hit both in deep water in winter."

--Wally Marshall, www.mrcrappie.com

Chapter VI

TACTICAL TIPS

Trolling for Crappie

My Uncle Guy taught me to troll for crappie. When I was young, my mother would wake me at 3 a.m. so I could rendezvous with him for a junket to the Mississippi River oxbows. We would arrive at one of the lakes in the dark and be fishing before daybreak.

I remember curtains of mist hanging over the water, and the croaking of coots in the buckbrush. I recall the traditional vittles—Vienna sausages, soda crackers and short Cokes—and the itchy butt I got from sitting too many hours on a too-hard boat seat. I recollect painted morning skies outlining galleries of cypress trees, and Uncle Guy's coffee-can spittoon perched precariously beside him in the homemade johnboat.

This angler has an ideal set-up for trolling: holders for several poles, an electric motor to help maintain the proper speed and a fish-finder at his feet that can be watched to enable trolling over good cover and structure. The result: crappie on the hook.

It's the fishing, though, I remember most. We looked, I'm sure, like a colossal spider blowing across the lake's surface, a dozen or more cane poles jutting from the sides of the boat as Uncle Guy sculled us across the lake. He knew all the honeyholes, and before long one of the poles would flex and bob, and one of us would pull a slab over the transom and place it in the fish basket. There were times when three poles would bend at once, and Uncle Guy would fuss at me in a gravel-voiced whisper, urging me to hurry—"Get them in, boy! Get them in!"—lest a big papermouth elude us. There were always plenty of fish to take home at day's end, and these jaunts with Uncle Guy grew into a lifelong passion for crappie fishing.

I still like trolling for crappie. I like it better than jigging jigs and dabbling minnows. Trolling lets you relax and enjoy the scenery. It's also among the best of all ways to find and catch crappie, no matter what time of year.

Tackle & Equipment

You can troll from the same boat you already use when crappie fishing. Use the same rods, reels, poles, line and other tackle already in service. Use one pole or a dozen, but determine beforehand if there are any restrictions. In some areas, you can fish with as many poles as you dare to; elsewhere, the number is limited.

If the wind's blowing, you can get by without a trolling motor, but you're not likely to catch as many crappie. Wind drifting is a one-way, time-consuming affair: make a drift, take up the poles, motor back up, reset the poles, drift again. An electric trolling motor allows constant fishing without fuss. It also permits you to vary your speed and control direction, important factors when chasing fussy crappie.

If you'll be using several poles (most trollers do), you need something to hold them at the ready. A few clamp-on rod holders fitted around the transom work ok. Or you can be more inventive. Some johnboat anglers use rigs called "trolling boards" to facilitate their efforts. Each is custom made by the angler to fit the particular style of boat being used. A board is cut to conform to the shape and size of the boat's front deck. Then several rod-holders are attached so the trolling poles will point in different directions in a half circle at the boat's bow. The trolling boards are clamped to the deck using C-clamps or bolts with wing nuts and can be easily removed.

When the trolling board is attached and the poles are in place, the boat looks like a big spider moving through the water with legs pointing in all directions. The angler usually starts by using a variety of baits rigged at different depths. For instance, if he's using six poles, four might be rigged with jigs in different colors and sizes, and the other two with minnows. Two baits might be set six feet deep, two at eight, and two at ten. This allows testing different baits and depths until you find actively feeding crappie. When you determine crappie favor a certain depth or bait, then all the poles are rigged to conform to that preference.

Anglers with bass boats sometimes mount two pedestal seats side-by-side on the front deck behind a wooden bar that holds six to eight rod holders. A sonar fish-finder also can be mounted on the bar, with the transducer attached to the trolling motor. With this setup, two anglers can experiment with different baits at different depths to quickly determine where crappie are holding.

Baits, Lures & Rigs

Jigs and live minnows entice crappie year-round, and most trollers stick to one, the other or a combination of the two. One popular trolling setup is a dragline rig, a multi-hook rig which is described in the chapter on "Overlooked Crappie Fishing Methods." In many cases, however, anglers prefer to simply use a single hook or lure on each line, or two hooks and lures rigged one above another using dropper loops.

Small spoons and spinners also work great in many situations, and crappie readily strike small baitfish-imitation crankbaits as well. One of my favorite trolling rigs uses a three-way swivel with a ⅛-ounce Luhr-Jensen Shyster spinner rigged above a Rebel Deep Wee R crankbait.

Speed

Speed probably is the most important aspect of trolling, but I don't know any magic formula for determining what speed is best under a given set of conditions. On some days you may have to inch your boat along to get strikes. On other days you must troll much faster to catch fish. And when you find the productive speed, you must maintain it, even when wind or current push your boat ahead or drive it back.

Savvy anglers experiment with different trolling speeds un-

Many trollers like to rig two lures on each line, each in a different color and/or size. When it's determined that one style is working best on crappie, then all the lures are changed to conform to that style.

til they determine what is most effective. This varies with the type of bait used and the measure of water clarity. For example, you might troll minnows or small spinners very slowly for crappie in a lake muddied by heavy rain. Crappie feed primarily by sight. In discolored water they may have a difficult time pinpointing a tiny, fast-moving jig but have little trouble homing in on a shiner or flashy spinnerbait slowly passing by.

In a clear-water lake, jigs may be very effective even at faster trolling speeds. Then again, they may not produce at all. The key word here is experiment. Try to figure how crappie are likely to react in the type water you're fishing, then adapt your tactics to conform to those expectations. But if your game plan doesn't produce within a short time, try something different. Sooner or later, the innovative crappie angler discovers a pattern for capitalizing on the situation.

One mistake crappie anglers often make is trolling at the same boat speed when headed into the wind as when headed with the wind. On an otherwise still lake, you travel faster with the wind than against it, assuming you never reposition your electric motor throttle. Therefore, in order to maintain your ideal trolling speed, you must adjust the throttle up or down depending on which way you are traveling.

The same is true when in current. When traveling against the flow, you must advance the throttle to maintain the same speed you had when traveling with the current. Fail to do so, and your speed will change dramatically. So will the number of crappie you're catching.

These factors may explain why you catch crappie when trolling in one direction and not in the other.

Off and Running

Some anglers start their troll blind; they have no idea what type of structure or cover is beneath the water. They simply start trolling and hope their hit-and-miss tactics produce more hits than misses.

It's best, however, to use sonar to pinpoint structure and cover crappie favor—woody cover along the edges of creek and river channels, long points, rock piles rising into lighted water, man-made fish attractors, etc.—and troll over that. With a serious look at a lake contour map and a quick check of prominent bottom changes with sonar, you could be catching slabs in minutes instead of wandering aimlessly.

Try zigzagging over channel breaks and adjacent flats. Stump fields and weed edges at proper depths may be good early and late when crappie are more likely to be feeding. In summer, crappie are likely to be strung out along the thermocline in a shallow plane, so covering large areas of water by trolling may enable you to catch more of these fish within a given range.

When you find schooling crappie, throw out a marker buoy so you can anchor just outside the school and cast to it, or continue to troll around the concentration. A savvy angler may take crappie from one of these marked spots for an hour or more, so long as the fish aren't spooked.

Crappie aren't hard to catch, but at times they're hard to find. Trolling, done properly, can help you overcome that problem. Hone your trolling skills to a fine edge and you'll rarely need to stop by the fish market on the way home.

Trolling Tips

- It's important to know how much line you have out when a crappie hits. When using spinning or spincasting equipment, after you set the hook, mark the line just in front of your reel using a waterproof felt marker. When you pay out line to that mark and troll through the area again, you know your bait will be at the same depth as before. Also, be sure to set your drag.
- The number of lines that can be trolled effectively depends to some degree on the experience of the angler. Experts sometimes can handle four or five rods, but most beginners should start with no more than two.
- How much line should you have out when trolling? When fishing jigs or minnows, most crappie anglers let out 50-75 feet. On windy days, they fish even farther back. The ideal distance varies with water clarity, speed, bait type and other factors. Experiment to see what works best.
- Let the motion of the boat do the hooksetting. Wait until the pole has a definite bend in it, then remove it from the holder and boat the fish. Don't stop the trolling motor. Before you get the first fish off, another may be on.

Many forms of superstructure can be seen in this photo of a lake that's been drawn down.

A Lesson on Superstructure

Structure is a word often bandied about in crappie-fishing circles. A man named Buck Perry coined the term decades ago and defined it as "an unusual change in the bottom contour of a lake or river."

Since then, fishermen have used the word structure to describe almost any type of cover or bottom feature one might chance upon during a day of fishing. Fallen timber, brush piles, stumps, boat docks, riprap, weed beds: you name it and someone will call it structure.

Savvy crappie anglers who want to catch lots of big slabs

know structure is the place to find fish. Crappie are highly object-oriented and almost always found near some type of cover or bottom anomaly that might, in the loosest sense of the term, be called structure.

Ardent crappie fishermen also have popularized another term designed to increase an angler's chance of locating crappie. This word is superstructure. An understanding of superstructure can take any crappie angler one step closer to success in the search for concentrations of fish.

Superstructure is a smaller, specific component of much larger structure where crappie are likely to gather. For example, if a submerged creek channel on a lake bottom is structure, then superstructure might be a short, timbered point jutting into a bend on that channel. If a boat dock is structure, a brush pile or abrupt drop-off adjacent the dock might be superstructure.

Similarly, if a large underwater hump is structure, crappie won't be evenly dispersed all around the hump. Instead, they'll be attracted to areas such as an isolated cluster of stumps, a tall bushy snag or any other feature distinctly different from the otherwise ordinary bottom feature. In other words, they're attracted to superstructure.

Lewis Peeler, a crappie fan from Wynne, Arkansas, learned about superstructure on a spring crappie fishing trip in Louisiana.

"A friend and I were jig fishing on a Mississippi River oxbow lake," he remembers. "A heavy rain had fallen the day prior to our arrival, and the crappie were gathered in mid-lake areas where isolated cypress trees towered over the water.

"There were several large solitary trees on the lake's north end, but crappie were not randomly scattered around them. We found the fish congregated in small, slightly deeper pockets of water situated near certain trees. We knew the crappie were probably in mid-lake haunts, but we had to refine our search to find the particular form of superstructure that attracted fish."

According to Peeler, fishing this lake was an important learning experience. "We'd work small tube jigs on one side of a tree and not get a nibble," he says. "Then we'd move them to the other side where our sonar indicated the water dropped abruptly from four to six feet. At that spot, we'd quickly catch a crappie. Prior to that day, before we understood the significance of superstructure, we might have jigged a few spots at a particular location then moved on, not realizing there were

A good sonar fishfinder is invaluable for pinpointing various types of super-structure that hold crappie.

probably plenty of slabs nearby but holding only around certain parts of the structure we were fishing.

"I've seen virtually the same situation in expansive spreads of flooded dead timber on big Southern reservoirs like those managed by the U.S. Army Corps of Engineers," Peeler continues. "As is often the case, you fish several hours without catching anything and eventually decide you must be dealing with crappie that have a serious case of lockjaw. Then, in one specific location that looks the same as scores of others you've already tried, you hook and land a dandy crappie. You remove the hook, and as you're tossing the fish in the livewell, your fishing buddy casts a little spinner and another slab wallops his lure. You start thinking, thank goodness they've started to bite. But likely as not, the crappie were biting all along. Up until this point, you just hadn't found them. They were holding near a small yet well-defined piece of superstructure. Perhaps there was a thick cluster of limbs still clinging to the side of one of the snags below the surface. Perhaps a different type of tree created superstructure. If the flooded timber was comprised primarily of tall oaks and hickories, the bushy skeleton of a single cedar tree on one edge would probably draw heavy concentrations of crappie. Pinpoint the particular type of superstructure the crappie are using and you'll start landing them one after another."

Peeler's experience brings to mind a small lake where I often fish. The lake only covers about 20 acres, so it's easy to fish the entire body of water in a one-day outing. A row of cypress trees running through the lake's mid-section provides the only available crappie cover, except for one little pocket at the end of the cypress row where there's a dense stand of button willows.

I've never been able to resist the temptation to jig around all the cypress trees, and on each visit, I'll pick up a few nice crappie around the knees of those trees. When I think back, though, I realize I've probably wasted a lot of time fishing around the cypress trees because over half the crappie I've caught in that lake have come from within that patch of button willows.

The same phenomenon regarding tree types often applies to boat docks as well. Boat docks attract lots of crappie, but not all boat docks. Some are better than others, and on lakes that have dozens of docks, the good docks might be considered a form of superstructure.

The docks most attractive to crappie are usually built on wood pilings, are in five to 15 feet of water near cover and/or structure, have been in the water several seasons, and lie very close to the water's surface. Docks meeting these criteria are extremely attractive to crappie because they provide shade throughout the day. The wood pilings provide a comfortable sense of security, which structure-oriented crappie require, and they also harbor a smorgasbord of foods. Algae growing on the seasoned wood hide grass shrimp, newly hatched minnows, aquatic insects, insect larvae and other crappie favorites.

Size is another consideration. Think of docks as fish hotels. Big hotels have rooms for lots of guests. Occupancy is limited, though, at smaller establishments. If other traits are equal, concentrate on large docks.

If you have a sonar unit on your boat, be sure to watch for brush piles placed around docks by the owners or local anglers. It's a rare instance when there aren't several brush piles in the

"When shooting docks, use light spinning tackle such as a Wally Marshall 4 foot, 6 inch Dock rod combo with 6-pound-test line and a 1/16-ounce Road Runner lure. Docks that have big sun decks, a lot of shade, night lights and mounted rod holders tell me the folks that own the dock are fishermen. Look for brush piles and vertical structure around the docks. Fish the darkest corner under the dock; it's the area where most crappie will hang out."
--Wally Marshall, www.mrcrappie.com

vicinity, and rare, too, when you won't find several nice crappie hiding within each of these shelters. Look, too, for nuances in bottom structure near docks that might concentrate fish—creek channels, deep pockets, small humps or other features.

Crappie anglers should also learn to distinguish between in-structures and out-structures. In-structures are always connected to the shore; out-structures are away from the shore, often in mid-lake or mid-stream.

One example of in-structure for crappie would be a long brush-covered point that gradually slopes into deeper water. A tree that has become uprooted and fallen over into the water would be in-structure, as would a fishing pier or anything else that is clearly part of the shoreline.

Out-structures include features such as inundated stream channels, humps, inundated ponds, saddles between islands, man-made fish attractors, timbered bars or any similar bottom feature well away from the shoreline.

The most important difference between these two fishing areas is that crappie generally use in-structures in spring and fall and out-structures in summer and winter. The only time crappie travel any appreciable distance is when they're making seasonal migrations from in-structures to out-structures or vice versa.

"This is important for crappie fisherman to know," says Peeler. "Each bit of superstructure where you find crappie should, if it remains unchanged, always attract crappie. But in most cases, crappie will only be found on that particular piece of superstructure during the proper season—on in-structure in spring and fall, on out-structure in summer and winter.

"You should still concentrate your attention on superstructure regardless of the season," he reports. "For example, if I'm fishing in-structure during the spring

Super-structure comes in two basic forms: in-structures, which touch the shore, and out-structures, which are away from the shore. Crappie generally use in-structures in spring and fall and out-structures in summer and winter.

spawning season, I'll look for something slightly different on the main structure that will concentrate crappie. A patch of green buckbrush may contain a log or cluster of stumps that draws crappie. If I'm fishing a brushy cove, I'll look for small points or other features along the perimeter where crappie are likely to hold. If I find crappie scattered here and there around cypress trees, I'll watch for unusual stands of knees that might tend to keep crappie more tightly schooled—knees in slightly deeper water or knees that are more tightly bunched together, things like that.

"Likewise, if I'm fishing around out-structure during summer and winter, I focus my attention on superstructure that shows up on my fish finder," he continues. "Primary creek channels are among the best structures to fish during these seasons, but crappie won't be found along the entire length of each channel. Instead, they'll be gathered in spots where the channel exhibits a change of some sort. This may be a bit of cover where a secondary channel intersects the main channel, or around a tall tree standing on a sharp bend in the channel—anything different from the norm. Finding these types of superstructure can mean the difference between catching lots of crappie or none at all."

Every good crappie fisherman knows the fundamentals of structure fishing. But if you want to improve your success rate even more, learn how to find and fish superstructure. This refined form of structure fishing will become the foundation for some of the best crappie fishing you've ever enjoyed.

Oxbow lakes are among the most scenic waters where crappie anglers can enjoy good fishing.

Understanding Oxbows

Word has it the crappie are tearing it up on a nearby oxbow lake. All week, a friend at the pool hall has been bragging about the cooler full of crappie he caught last Saturday. The fishing report in yesterday's newspaper said several 2-pounders were weighed in earlier this week, and limit stringers have been common.

You heard similar reports this time last year but never found time to make the long drive. No such misfortune now, though, so you hitch up the boat, pick up your fishing pal Bubba, and at dawn, the two of you have your first glimpse of this 1,000-acre natural lake.

Everything looks perfect. It's been raining to the north for several days, but the skies here are just overcast. You're a bit surprised there aren't more folks out fishing, but, hey, that just makes things all the better.

As the sun sets, you arrive back at the boat ramp. "I just don't understand it," Bubba whines. "Just a few days ago, Mack was over here and loaded the boat with some dandy crappie. We get here and nothing . . . not even a nibble."

Has something similar to this ever happened to you? For many inexperienced anglers, catching crappie in an oxbow lake is like attempting to break a secret code. Try as they might, it seems impossible to achieve success, and many go away frustrated, vowing never again to fish an oxbow.

Contrary to the opinions of some unfortunate fishermen, the only real secret to oxbow crappie fishing is preparing yourself with an in-depth knowledge of oxbow dynamics. In many physical respects, oxbows are vastly different than man-made lakes, and each oxbow has characteristics that make it different from other oxbows. Unless one knows and understands these differences, fishing for crappie may be nothing more than a waterhaul.

What the fellows in our opening story didn't know was that upstate rains had caused the adjoining river to overflow into the oxbow 48 hours prior to their arrival. Yes, folks were catching lots of crappie a few days earlier, and by all appearances, it should have been a decent day for fishing. But a sharp rise in the water level, unnoticeable to our fishing duo, gave crappie a bad case of lockjaw. Few fishermen were on the lake that day because most regulars knew of the impending rise and knew crappie weren't likely to bite until conditions stabilized.

Rapidly changing water levels are just one of several factors oxbow anglers must figure into the crappie-angling equation. To better understand the variables that influence oxbow crappie fishing, let's examine the origins and physical attributes of oxbow lakes. Knowing what to look for, and when and where, will increase your odds for success.

Oxbow Origins

A lowland river left to its own devices will writhe and twist in its valley like a head-shot snake. The river erodes earth away in one place only to deposit it somewhere else, and though a river may always look the same to a casual visitor, it's never the same two days in a row.

Many small oxbow lakes have limited access and thus little fishing pressure. Crappie grow huge as a result.

Over the years, a lowland river plows a new channel here and abandons an old one there, always following the path of least resistance. Sometimes, when a meandering stream erodes the shores of its broad bends, loops of water are severed from the main stream. The ends of the loops are blocked by sediments deposited by the parent stream, and a crescent-shaped lake is left behind. The shape of these lakes resembles the U-shaped piece of wood on an ox yoke, and thus they are called oxbow lakes. Oxbow lakes are also known as cutoffs or river lakes.

When an oxbow is cut off from the river, its character immediately begins changing. The absence of continually flowing water allows sediment carried in from seasonal flooding to build up on the bottom, and the old meander scar becomes shallower and relatively flat-bottomed. Water-tolerant plants such as cypress, tupelo and willows take root along the lake's edges. In years of drought, some shallow oxbows dry up, allowing plants to gain a foothold and encroach still farther into the lake. It's because of this cyclic process that many oxbows have large cypress trees growing in the middle of the lake, or have a ring of living trees and shrubs extending 50 to 100 feet or more out from dry land.

All these natural processes, from the natural cutting off of a new oxbow to the building up of bottom sediment to the gradual extension of woody vegetation farther and farther from the bank, are stages in the death of an oxbow lake. The process may take 500 years or more, but left undisturbed, all oxbows will eventually silt in and transform into wetland forest.

During this long process of dying, oxbows can provide fantastic crappie fishing. The annual cycle of winter/spring flooding that gradually chokes these lakes with silt also figures heavily in making them the outstanding crappie fisheries they are.

The annual flooding cycle stimulates oxbow crappie to go on a feeding binge as waters recede to normal levels. The feeding binge puts them in excellent spawning condition, and because oxbows are very fertile, heavy spawns usually follow each winter/spring flooding cycle. Spawning still occurs in years of low rain, when flooding is absent, but it doesn't happen with the gusto that characterizes post-flood spawns.

Oxbow Types

Mastering oxbow crappie fishing requires knowledge of the various types of oxbow lakes. Some oxbows remain connected to the parent stream; some are not. Some lie within the floodplain of major streams, while others lie entirely outside the floodplain. Differing conditions on each type of oxbow dictate the manner and amount of planning necessary to enjoy a productive crappie fishing trip.Oxbows that remain connected to their parent river during all or part of the year normally provide the best fishing for big crappie. When the connecting river floods the oxbow, inflowing nutrients enrich the water and help sustain thriving communities of forage animals on which crappie feed. This yearly overflow cycle also provides temporary, but important, spawning habitat for oxbow crappie.

Unfortunately, severe water level fluctuations also make river-connected oxbows the trickiest to fish. When the river rises to a certain level, the lake also rises. When the river falls, the lake falls. Changing water conditions dramatically affect fishing, and anglers must monitor water levels closely to pick the most productive days.

There are no hard-and-fast rules for fishing river-connected oxbows; fish are caught under all conditions. But as a general rule, crappie seldom bite when the water is on a fast rise. Fishing run-out areas—the cuts connecting oxbow and river—can sometimes be outstanding during a fast fall. But the best fishing on these oxbows is usually when the water level is steady or slowly rising or falling.

On river-connected oxbows, crappie anglers should also know the depth at which the river moves in and out of the oxbow being fished. This information is usually available at local bait shops or from area anglers, and once you know it, you can monitor the river level in local newspapers or via government hotlines or websites to plan a trip during peak fishing periods. When the river is entirely out of the oxbow, water conditions, and thus fishing conditions, are likely to be more stable and predictable. When the river overflows into the oxbow, anglers must know the intensity of water level fluctuations—fast rise, slow fall, etc.—to determine the best crappie fishing days.

Many oxbows are no longer connected to the river proper but still lie within the stream floodplain. These lakes are still subject to flooding and rapidly changing water levels during wet months, and here again, crappie anglers should scrutinize water fluctuations when planning a visit.

Some oxbows lie outside the river floodplain, completely isolated by levees or dams. These lakes usually provide the most predictable fishing opportunities because water fluctuations are less dramatic and have less influence on overall fishing conditions. Consequently, they may be the best oxbows to fish when water conditions are unfavorable elsewhere. If it's big crappie you seek, however, you'll probably be disappointed. The absence of an annual overflow cycle leads to decreased fertility, and quality crappie—1½- to 3-pounders—are seldom found.

These general guidelines can be helpful, but don't neglect to do additional homework before fishing. Some isolated oxbows offer astounding fishing for trophy-class crappie, and some river-connected lakes may produce few, if any, crappie. Prepare yourself by contacting local bait shop proprietors or fisheries biologists and asking a few basic questions. Is this a good crappie lake during this time of year? What size crappie are likely to be caught? Can you offer pointers on picking the best fishing days? Can you suggest where I might call for an up-to-date report on fishing conditions? The more you know about a lake before you visit, the better your chances for success.

Finding Oxbow Crappie

Finding oxbow crappie isn't unusually complicated. Work all available cover carefully, probing every nook and cranny in the brush and every likely log and cypress tree, changing baits and presentations until you find what works best.

Dipping jigs and minnows around shallow cover is a good way to zero in on oxbow crappie.

One thing to remember is that even though most oxbows are relatively flat and of uniform depth, the outside bend of the lake is almost always a little deeper than the inside bend. This can be important when water temperatures rise above the crappie's 70 to 75 degree comfort range. When this happens, crappie tend to concentrate on the lake's deeper side where the temperature is more to their liking. In most oxbows, the amount of deep water is very limited, so you don't have to look far to find fish.

When crappie are in the shallows, they invariably relate to some sort of cover. Cypress trees skirt the banks of many oxbows, and working jigs or minnows around their broad bases and knees is a good way to catch crappie. Buckbrush and willows are also prevalent in many oxbows, and many crappie are caught in the thickest such cover available. Other prime fishing spots include fallen trees, beaver lodges, sunken Christmas tree shelters, lily pads, weed beds, shoreline riprap, stump fields, boat docks and duck hunting blinds.

If you're on an oxbow when flood waters are receding, try fishing around run-out chutes between oxbow and river. These are crappie magnets that attract fish with the promise of an easy meal. Look for areas where out-flowing water is constricted, such as sloughs and natural cuts, then work a minnow, jig or jig/spinner combo around surrounding woody cover. Key your efforts to periods when water is falling three to six inches a day; a faster fall makes it hard to locate fish.

One final note: when you're considering where to go, think small. Although some oxbows cover several thousand acres, the real jewels are much smaller. It's harder to pinpoint crappie in the larger oxbows, and fishing them isn't much different than fishing the nearest Corps of Engineers mega-lake.

For the true oxbow experience, visit small lakes off the beaten path. It's not uncommon to fish all day on one of these little oxbows and never see another boat. The splendid bottomland scenery will take you back to a time when our country was still wild and uncharted, and you'll experience a feeling of wonderment and tranquility no man-made impoundment can impart. When the crappie are biting, there's only one way to describe it: heaven on earth.

The run-out chute between an oxbow lake and its parent river often is a crappie magnet.

Understanding oxbow lakes and how to fish them will add a whole new dimension to your fishing. Hopefully, the facts presented here will help you get off to a good start, so you, too, can enjoy the magic and majesty of these blue-ribbon crappie lakes.

W.T. and Curt Moore often bury their boat in thicket cover to get at the trophy-size crappie that like to lurk in these locales.

Hideaway Crappie

Curt Moore smiles as he holds up an almost 2-pound crappie, pretends to kiss it, then carefully places the fish into a basket already full of jumbo slabs.

"Luck," his father, W.T., says from the back of the boat, a twinge of envy in his voice. "Just pure dumb luck."

Undaunted, Curt returns to the business at hand, maneuvering a jig back into a tract of flooded buckbrush that's thick enough to hide a hunter-orange hippo. Carefully guiding his pole through the maze of cover, he finds a hole about as big as the rim of a coffee mug, then lowers the tiny lure below the surface. It falls only a foot or so before the pole arcs downward, and Curt yanks yet another big crappie from its down-under hidey-hole.

"Luck, huh?" Curt says snidely, swinging the fish back in front of his dad's face. "You call that..."

But before he can get the words out, W.T. is tussling with his own buckbrush crappie. For a moment, it appears the fish will tangle him up and escape. But pulling it quickly to his rod tip, W.T. manages to pluck the silvery prize from the grasp of the gnarly bushes. The crappie is half again the size of the one Curt has just landed.

"Keep after those baby fish if you want to, son," W.T. says, grinning. "But when you're finished playing around, turn around here, and I'll show you how to catch the big ones."

The comments on luck and skill are made in jest. W.T. knows better than anyone that luck has little to do with the number of big crappie his son is catching. And Curt knows his dad is anything but a pushover when it comes to boating heavyweight slabs.

These two Mountain View, Arkansas men have spent thousands of hours fishing together, and with years of on-the-water experience under their belts, both have developed an uncanny knack for finding and catching big crappie. When other anglers are complaining because the fish aren't biting, they're pulling dozens of hefty "specks" over the transom.

How do they do it? Much of their success can be attributed to their unique style of fishing. You see, when this father-and-son team go after big crappie, they don't just fish cover, they immerse themselves in it. Pushing and pulling their johnboat over, under, around and through buckbrush, willows, treetops and other seemingly impenetrable crappie habitat, they eventually wind up right in the thick of it, nearly hidden from view.

Passing boaters often call out, offering to help extract them from their tangly predicament, for most cannot fathom the fact that anyone in their right mind would purposely place themselves in such a deplorable situation. They would find it even harder to believe these guys are actually fishing, and quite successfully at that.

Looking at the dense tangles of crappie cover the Moores often fish, most anglers would pass it by without a second glance, opting for more accessible spots in which to dangle their offerings. That's exactly why this pair fishes where they do. They've learned that angler-shy crappie instinctively seek the sanctuary of thick cover off the beaten path, and this is

The intertangled branches of beaver lodges often are home to slab crappie.

where the biggest fish—crappie a pound and up—are most likely to be found. Using long poles to work jigs in the heart of extremely dense stands of brush and vegetation, they catch extraordinary numbers of trophy-size crappie, even under the toughest fishing conditions.

"If you pass up heavy cover because it looks too hard to fish, you're probably passing up lots of nice crappie," Curt says. "There's usually a lot of fishing traffic on the outer edges of cover, but few anglers try to get into the center, so there are likely to be more fish there.

"Big crappie don't get big by being stupid. They're going to hide where few anglers go. That's why you find so many nice fish way back in the brush."

"It's a lot of work trying to get your boat back into these areas," he says. "And when you start fishing, you're going to get hung up a lot and lose a lot of lures and a lot of fish. That can be extremely frustrating.

"Still, nothing is more frustrating than not catching fish," he adds. "We start out fishing the outer edges of cover, just like most crappie fishermen. But if the fishing's slow, we head for the thickest, out-of-the-way cover we can find, places other fishermen are passing by. That's where the crappie, especially big crappie, are going to be. And if we lose a few ... well, that's just part of the game. Better to catch some and lose some than not to catch any at all."

Of course, there's more to catching hideaway crappie than just finding a big thicket and barging in. For starters, anglers must know how to pinpoint crappie within large swaths of dense, unbroken habitat. Some locales offer distinctly better possibilities than others.

"You want to look for something that sets itself apart from the predominant cover," says W.T. "Look back into the brush and try to find a stump, a log, some downed timber. That's where you want to fish.

"The best areas also have some type of structure beneath the cover," he says. "Look for heavy cover over points, near steep banks or anywhere the water drops fairly quickly from

156 THE CRAPPIE BOOK

shallow to deep. In these areas, you can fish a variety of depths until you find the level where crappie are holding."

Getting into these jungle-like areas isn't easy, and anglers fishing from large, heavy bass boats will find it almost impossible. The Moores opt for a light, narrow, 12-foot aluminum johnboat outfitted with a small outboard, no trolling motor and a minimum of fishing tackle.

"You don't want a bunch of heavy gear holding you back," Curt says. "You have to get away from the outside edge and back into the thicket to find the best crappie, and the only way to do that is to grab hold of limbs and pull your way through until you can reach the spot where you want to fish."

All this activity creates noise that would seem intolerable to big crappie. But these popular sportfish will abide more clamor than most anglers realize.

"You don't want to be excessively noisy," W.T. says, "but noise doesn't seem to bother crappie that much, especially spawning crappie. You can pull your boat up on that brush, breaking and snapping, then just drop a jig in and catch a fish. Even though you may think pulling your boat in there is going to run all the crappie out, that's not necessarily the case."

When you're in a thicket, you must have the proper equipment to fish it. Both men recommend a long jigging pole rigged with heavy line.

"I prefer a long pole so I can reach out," explains Curt. "Instead of having a 10-foot pole, use a 12 or 15 to give you extra reach. That way you can fish a larger area before you have to move the boat."

W.T. recommends using a graphite pole for lightness and sensitivity.

"Graphite is sensitive," he says, "so it helps you better detect the strikes of light-biting crappie. But more importantly, graphite is light. If you use graphite, you don't wear your arm out holding up a heavy pole. That's important to remember when you're planning to fish all day with a long jigging pole."

Seventeen-pound-test line is the Moore standard.

"You need heavier line in the brush," W.T. says. "If you hang a pound-and-a-half crappie, you've got to hoss him out of there or he's going to wrap and break off on you. You must have heavier line to do that. And unless the water is extremely clear, I don't think larger-diameter line affects the number of crappie you'll hook when fishing heavy cover."

Many anglers fish the edges of thickets. The smart ones also learn to fish the interiors of these crappie hideouts, regardless of the difficulties involved.

Though many anglers prefer minnows for enticing crappie, a live bait swimming at the end of your line compounds the problem of hangups when fishing thickets. Jigs, on the other hand, are ideal for fishing tiny pockets of water in mazes of interlocking brush and timber. Any standard crappie jig will work, but the Moores fish almost exclusively with $1/32$-ounce leadheads dressed with rubber tube skirts.

"Fishing heavy cover is intimidating the first time you try it," says W.T. "You worry about hangups, and you worry about losing fish. You wonder how in the world you can even get your line out there without tangling it on a limb. With jigs, though, it's really not as bad as you might think if you use the right technique.

"I use a 12 foot jigging pole with eyes on it like a fly rod," he continues. "I start by grabbing my line just below the bottom eye, and pull the jig up to my rod tip. Then I work the rod back where I want to go and let the jig down. When a fish hits, you pull it out the same way. Keep the line in your hand, set the hook, pull the fish up to the rod tip as fast as you can so it can't tangle you, then back your rod up to get the fish in the boat."

"Big crappie like to hide in spots of real tight cover," Curt adds. "That makes it hard to fish with a minnow below a bobber because you have line dangling from your rod tip, and the minnow is constantly moving around, getting you hung up.

"If you use a jig, though, you can pull it all the way up to the rod tip, work it back in the brush carefully, then let it down through a hole in the brush. The hole doesn't have to be big for you to fish it with a jig—about the size of silver dollar, if that big. And though you wouldn't think you could pull a 2-pound crappie out of a hole that size, you can. Most of the time anyway. You're going to lose some fish, but usually, if you get a good hookset and hoss that fish up and out of the brush, you can get him in the boat."

The underlying key to the Moores' success is fishing out-of-the-way areas other anglers pass by. But this doesn't always require dragging a boat into tight-knit stands of cover.

"Using a long pole, you can reach places other people don't fish, even without pulling your boat back in the brush," W.T. says. "For instance, if a bank is lined with brush that extends 15 feet out from the shore, you'll catch a lot of crappie other folks miss just by reaching back deeper in that brush with a jig. Don't overlook places like this."

Another Moore tactic is simply to fish waters where few anglers go. "One of my favorite crappie spots is a stream in east Arkansas," Curt says. "I usually fish where there's not as much boat traffic, way up the creek. That's where I usually have the best luck. And if you know where you're going, you can pull your boat out of the creek and drag it 50 yards and you'll be in some oxbow lakes that very seldom see a boat. In spots like this that don't get much fishing pressure, you can tear the crappie up."

A long jigging pole provides the ideal means for getting at crappie in dense, hard-to-fish cover.

No matter where you fish, applying the tactics shared by these two crappie experts can improve your catch.

Don't get the wrong idea, though. Catching hideaway crappie isn't a lark. Fishing heavy cover successfully requires hard work and patience.

"Look at it this way, " says W.T. "When fishing is slow, you can take the easy way out and go home empty-handed, or you can work a little harder and catch some real nice crappie. What's it gonna be?"

Sling-shotting a jig is a good way to get at crappie beneath low docks and other man-made structures.

Overlooked Crappie Fishing Methods

Stick to traditional approaches when they're producing crappie. But when "normal" tactics won't work, the following often-overlooked methods can make your catch rate soar.

Draglining

Draglining—trolling with a bottom-weighted crappie rig—is an excellent method for pinpointing hard-to-find slabs holding in deep water along creek channels, humps and other bottom structure. Attach a 1-ounce bank sinker to the end of your main line. Above this are two to four 12-inch-long drop lines spaced about 18 inches apart. Each drop line is connected to the main line via a loop knot or swivel. Jigs, minnows, jig/minnow combos or a combination of these are tied to the drops.

While wind drifting or slow trolling with an electric motor, work the rig vertically beside the boat using a "lift, drop" action. When you feel the rig bump against cover or structure, raise it up and over. The angler must be attentive at all times, raising or lowering the rig with the rod tip in order to maintain "feel" with the rig below and keep it bouncing across the pieces of cover and structure without hanging. Strikes often come just as the rig is lowered behind woody cover.

Stump-knocking

Good crappie lakes often contain big stands of flooded cypress trees. Crappie seek shelter in the convoluted folds around the bases of big cypresses or in clusters of knees encircling the trees. You can use a jigging pole or long cane pole to work your lure in and around this cover, but if the fish are skittish, it may be difficult to approach close enough to use a pole without spooking them.

To solve this problem, try a tactic Southern anglers call stump-knocking. Remain at a distance, and use an ultralight spinning or spincast combo to cast a jig or jig/spinner combo right up against the side of the tree. Cast right at the tree, and let the lure smack into the trunk and roll off into the water below.

Crappie usually hold right beside the tree in hollows and folds, waiting to ambush passing baitfish or watching for insects to tumble off the branches overhead. Most will strike as soon as the lure tumbles into the water, but if you don't get a hit right off, retrieve the lure and try other spots.

Sling-shotting

When crappie are hiding beneath man-made structures such as docks, piers and boathouses, try sling-shotting to get at them. This technique uses a short fishing rod like a sling-shot to catapult a crappie jig into the shady area beneath the structure.

Use a 4½ to 5½ foot, medium-action rod outfitted with a spincasting reel or an autocast spinning reel that allows you to pick up the line and flip the bail at the same time. A $1/32$-ounce jig is right for most situations, and you're better off using solid-body jigs when sling-shotting because they stay on better

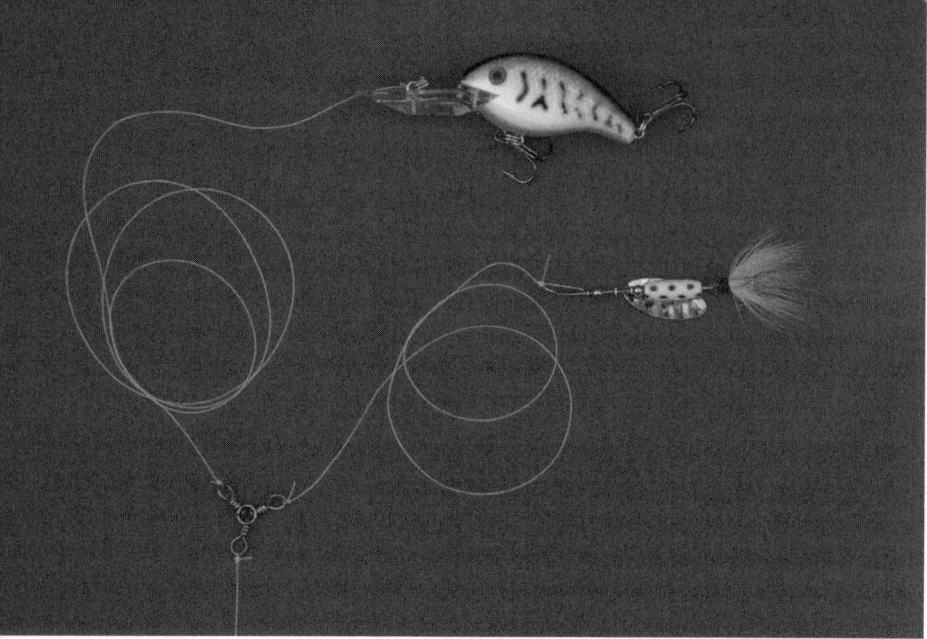

This combination rig—a Rebel Wee R crankbait and Luhr-Jensen Shyster spinnerbait—often is used by double-dipping crappie anglers when trolling.

than tube jigs. Pinch the jig carefully between the thumb and index finger of your free hand, pull the rod back like a bow, aim and release the lure, letting it fly beneath the structure. With some practice, you can sling-shot a small jig 15 to 20 feet under a dock or boathouse where big crappie are hiding.

Prepare for a strike as the lure falls. It helps to use highly visible line so you can see slight line movements that signal a taker. No hits? A slow retrieve close to the bottom frequently produces.

Double-dipping

Double-dippers use various lure/bait combinations to increase their odds for catching crappie. For example, one of my favorite trolling rigs is a ⅛-ounce Luhr-Jensen Shyster spinner rigged above a Rebel Deep Wee R crankbait. Tie the spinner to a 12-inch leader and the crankbait to a 24-inch leader. Then tie each leader to a separate eye on a three-swivel, and tie the other swivel eye to your main line. Now you're ready to troll, and chances are, you'll hook two fish at a time more than once.

If you pinpoint feeding crappie near schools of surface-running shad, try casting a ¹⁄₃₂ ounce jig tied above a ⅛-ounce jig with a small safety-pin spinner. The heavier jig stays well beneath the upper lure at a level where larger crappie are often holding. Double hookups are common.

Experiment with various combinations. You'll probably be surprised how effective double-dipping can be.

Dock-walking

Summer crappie may move fairly shallow, even on sunny days, if they can find overhead cover that shades them from bright rays. Boat docks, fishing piers and swimming platforms provide such cover, but anglers in boats may fail to get bites because crappie can see them. These same fish may bite, however, when the angler walks on the wooden structure and fishes from above. Crappie get used to foot traffic on these structures and seldom spook, so the quiet overhead approach often works when a bait presented from a boat won't. Let the wind drift a minnow or jig suspended under a bobber into the shade beneath the structure. Or try fishing vertically through wide cracks in boards that lie over the shadiest water.

Next time the crappie aren't biting, give these tactics a try. They can be every bit as effective as the old reliables.

Pro Tip

"Do fish scents make a difference? Is the sense of smell important to crappie anglers using both live bait and artificial jigs? Yes.

"After logging long hours and many days back to back on the lake in my years as a professional guide, I've seen strange things happen. I've had clients fishing side by side in the boat with identical rigs only to have one consistently catch fish while the other struggled.

"I've found positive results when tipping jigs with Berkley's Power Bait Crappie Nibbles, Fish Formula's liquid scents and Kodiak Fish Attractant gel.

"Crappie seem to take the bait better and hold on to it longer when using such fish attractants."

--Steve McCadams, www.stevemccadams.com

TROPHY TACTICS

One Guide's Secrets for Giant Crappie

An angler who consistently catches crappie must possess many positive attributes. He must have an in-depth knowledge of crappie behavior. He must know where crappie are likely to be found throughout the seasons and under a wide variety of weather and water conditions. He must know the best baits and lures for enticing his quarry in each body of water he fishes, and the right ways to present those enticements so crappie want to eat them.

When your vocation is crappie fishing, it's even more important to be in tune with the ways of these popular panfish. In addition, you must be able to quickly adapt to changing or unfamiliar conditions. Because your livelihood depends on your abil-

Todd Huckabee shows an impressive stringer of crappie that fell for Yum Wooly Beavertails worked around schools of threadfin shad.

ity to put fish in the boat, you need enough tricks up your sleeve to make this happen even under the worse circumstances. In other words, you need to be flexible and innovative—ready to try something new or different when "regular" fishing tactics won't produce.

This latter group of anglers includes tournament pros and fishing guides, and in a few rare instances, people like Todd Huckabee of Oklahoma City, Oklahoma, who make their living doing both. I've been fortunate to fish with several such individuals, but I can say without reservation, none comes close to Huckabee when it comes to flexibility and innovation. This crappie expert is always thinking "outside the box," and has developed several slab-hooking techniques that are out-of-the-ordinary, yet astoundingly productive for heavyweight fish.

Huckabee spends an average of 270 days annually fishing for crappie. As a full-time crappie guide, he fishes with clients on several Oklahoma lakes about 150 days each year.

Huckabee also is a respected tournament professional. He qualified for the Crappie USA Classic in 2004 and 2005, and for the CAST (Crappie Angler Sportsman Tour) Classic in 2003, 2004 and 2005.

Few anglers are more qualified to give advice on catching big slabs and lots of them. And Huckabee kindly agreed to share some of his secrets for waylaying out-sized crappie. The tips that follow could help you catch some of the biggest crappie you've ever seen.

Facts About Shad, Brush Piles and Big Crappie

In March 2003, Todd Huckabee invited me to join him for a crappie fishing trip on Oklahoma's Eufaula Lake, a 102,000-acre Corps of Engineers impoundment 12 miles east of Eufaula in McIntosh County.

"We have two basic choices," he said when I arrived. "We can try to catch a lot of crappie, or we can focus on catching trophy-size crappie."

I chose the latter, figuring Huckabee would head for some hidden brush piles or other fish attractors like most guides with whom I've fished. To my surprise, that was not the case.

Huckabee explained that in Eufaula Lake and other waters with abundant schools of threadfin shad, big crappie are more likely to be found near schools of shad than holding around brush piles. Unlike small crappie, which find a safe haven from predators in a brush pile's maze of branches, these 2-pound-plus giants aren't on the menu of many meat-eaters. Their own appetite is substantial, however, so they follow roaming shad schools, feasting on these high-protein baitfish to fuel their internal furnaces.

"Lots of brush piles placed in an area may actually keep big crappie away," said Huckabee. "The schools of shad these big crappie feed on prefer open waters without obstructions that block their movements. If brush piles are in the area, the fish must go around them. They don't like this, so they avoid these areas. You'll catch more and bigger crappie if you fish near underwater ledges, ripraped banks or even the bottom where shad are schooling."

Huckabee flipped on his depthfinder and showed me a compact band of pixels running across the screen that indicated a big school of threadfins 10 feet below the boat. Crappie appeared as scattered blips around and beneath the shad. Find this signature, Huckabee said, and you can target the crappie with lures appropriate to the situation.

Dippin' Crappie

According to Oklahoma City crappie guide Todd Huckabee, on some crappie lakes, there's a saying among tournament anglers: "The guy that dips the most trees win."

Dippin' is a way of fishing standing timber in water as deep as 20 feet.

"This tactic works best in areas with 'slick' timber," Huckabee says. "By that, I mean timber that's pretty much just like a telephone pole. I believe bigger crappie like this better because they can move around it better. Crappie a pound or less prefer to have some branches or brush but the larger crappie don't." The lure Huckabee uses for dippin' is a Yum Wooly Beavertail or Yum Vibra King Tube on a 3/16-ounce jighead.

"I drop the lure next to the timber and either catch a fish or move on to the next pole," Huckabee says. "The secret is to let the lure sit for 10 seconds to a minute before ever moving it. If you don't have a bite by then, move the lure up very slowly in a controlled fashion. Fish it slowly all the way around the pole, then move to the next pole."

Huckabee says dippin' works year-round except during the spawn or during real high water.

"You may have to come back and fish around the same pole five times before a fish will hit," he notes. "I think the crappie sometimes leave their pole to go feed, then return to rest. And after you finally catch one, there may not be another fish on the same pole that day."

"Bigger baits, slick structure and repeated offerings": those are keys for dippin' slabs, says Huckabee.

Tackle Tips

"Big crappie feeding on big baitfish often ignore the $1/64$- to $1/16$-ounce jigs many crappie anglers use," Huckabee told me. "Trophy-class crappie like to fill their bellies with one big bite, not several little ones, so I use lures that are much larger than those other fishermen typically tie on."

The lures in this case were two-inch Yum Wooly Beavertails on $1/8$-ounce Crappie Pro jigheads. Huckabee pinched off the head of each soft-plastic lure, then rigged two on each line about 18 inches apart, each on a dropper loop.

"If shad are eight to 10 feet deep," he said, "position the jigs so they'll be at eight to 10 feet during a slow troll. Maintain a boat speed that keeps your line perpendicular to the water's surface. Slightly lift and drop the rig as you move, maintaining a feel of the bottom as the weight bumps along."

Huckabee's rod of choice is Zebco's 8- or 10-foot Slab Seeker.

"These are made out of Z-glass and have Tap Action Tips," said Huckabee. "The tip is extremely small in diameter. It will collapse during the hookset so you're actually setting the hook with the next guide down for more hooksetting power, yet you still having a very soft sensitive tip."

Zebco spincast and spinning reels with Depth Locator Technology also are Huckabee standards.

"These reels allow you to place your lure at the same depth over and over again," he said. "That's very important. For example, if I'm fishing in 20-26 feet of water and the crappie are 19 feet deep, the lure must go back to 19 feet each time. With these reels, I can move from one spot to another, and my clients or I can drop a jig to the correct depth without any hassle."

Huckabee also uses a product called the Stabor Line Lock.

"This handy little device enables me to put different jigs on

Yum Wooly Beavertail

without retying," he said. "You just wrap the line around the shank and pull it through the eye without tying a knot. And you can remove it just as easy and fish just one jig."

As we fished Eufaula Lake, Huckabee kept his eyes on the sonar, and we kept our Beavertail rigs working in and around the shad schools. Whenever we reached the edge of a school, Huckabee turned the boat and trolled through the school again. Typically, we caught two or more crappie on each pass. All these were true trophy-class fish. During four hours working open-water shad schools, I caught 17 crappie. The smallest weighed two pounds, one ounce. The rest were slightly larger.

Crankbait Crappie

Keeping with Huckabee's "bigger is better" lure theme, you might try a big crankbait to entice deep summer slabs. Huckabee innovated a technique that employs a Carolina-rigged Smithwick Rogue (4½-inch suspending model, shad-like colors) to catch 2-pound-plus crappie.

"When big crappie go deep in winter, their metabolism stays pretty high," he said. "These fish are preparing for the spawn, and they're eating a lot. But during summer, these same deepwater crappie are kind of lazy. If you drop a lure like a Beavertail down to them, often it's just not enough to entice them. They really don't seem interested in eating something unless it's bigger. That's why I use the Rogue.

"You make this rig with a ⅛- to ¼-ounce tungsten weight above a barrel swivel on the main line," Huckabee continued. "Then tie a three- to foot-foot leader from the swivel to the crankbait. Cast it out, let it sink, then just crawl the lure across the bottom. Big crappie that won't dart out after smaller prey find it hard to resist a big meal like this."

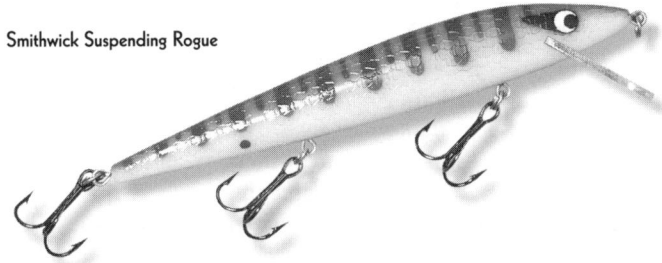

Smithwick Suspending Rogue

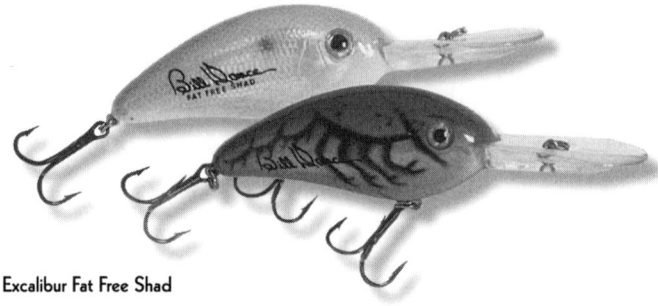

Excalibur Fat Free Shad

Huckabee often fishes with another modified crankbait rig as well. This one employs Excalibur's Fat Free Shad or Fat Free Guppy.

"I modify each lure by removing the back treble hook and placing a crappie tube skirt on the hook's shank," said Huckabee. "The hook is then replaced. The skirt works just like the feathers on some topwater plugs, giving the lure more action. I like to alternate colors of the components. For example, I might use a crankbait that has a citrus-shad color and add a pink skirt. This seems more effective than using components with similar colors."

Huckabee uses this rig to target crappie when they're feeding on threadfin shad around shoreline riprap and rocks.

"The shad often are right up on the rocks where you can see them," he says. "The crappie position themselves beneath the baitfish, usually in five or six feet of water. I fish the Fat Free crankbaits just like I might fish them for bass—working them parallel to the bank, cranking them down to the rocks and making contact with the bottom. Then I slow the lure down and just wait for a big crappie to strike."

During a typical year Huckabee may catch more 200 crappie, each exceeding two pounds, using this rig.

Shallow Summer Crappie

During the blistering 100-degree days often seen in late summer, most anglers seek crappie in deep-water haunts. Once again, Huckabee breaks the mold.

"I've learned to look for big crappie up on shallow [one to three foot deep] flats in creeks this time of year," he said. "Shad spawn over and over again in these areas as long as conditions are right. And the big crappie follow them. The crappie are always next to some piece of cover such as a laydown, a log jam or a standing stump. And flats where cover is sparse are best because, on these, any little stick will hold fish. The water needs to be stained."

Huckabee discovered trophy crappie in these locales while bass fishing, and decided to experiment with different fishing techniques until he found one that worked best.

"The best lure in this situation seems to be a two-inch, black/pink Yum Wooly Beavertail on a ³⁄₁₆-ounce Crappie Pro jig head," he said. "And I found that the crappie tend to hold near one particular kind of cover each day. One day they may be on laydowns, and I catch more if I work that cover. The next day they may be on log jams or stumps, and working the Beavertail around that cover is more productive."

Huckabee also targets big summer crappie in flooded willows. Here again, the rig he uses is somewhat different from the rigs selected by most crappie anglers.

"I catch a ton of post-spawn crappie by wacky-rigging a 3-inch Yum Dinger and fishing it around water willows and around shallow brush close to docks. They can't resist the slow fall and wiggle of a Dinger that's rigged this way with the hook run through the center of the lure. The four-inch Dingers work, too, but I found I get a better hooking ratio with the smaller lure. This is a fun way to fish because of the numbers of other crappie you catch."

More Innovations

It seems like every time I talk with Todd, he's come up with another new tactic that's dynamite on giant crappie. His bag of tricks runs deep already, but he's continually studying crappie behavior and experimenting with new lures and new ways of fishing that will give him an edge on tournament competitors and make him a better guide.

If you, too, want to be a better crappie angler, I suggest you follow his lead. Don't get stuck in a rut. Think outside the box occasionally. Innovation often leads to success.

Yum Dinger

The Smithwick Rogue presents a large target for hungry but lethargic crappie holding deep in summer.

Tips for Catching Trophy Crappie

How can you catch your biggest crappie ever? Many anglers want a simple answer to that question—a magic pill, a silver bullet, some tight-lipped secret the anglers who are consistently catching trophy crappie must know about but won't tell. Unfortunately, there's not one. But there are proven tactics you can employ that are likely to add up to eventual success. Here are some to get you started.

Fish the Best Waters

All waters are not created equal. You'll home in on a trophy quicker if you choose those proven to produce extra-large crappie, even if it means traveling. Contact your state fisheries department or a local fisheries biologist for information that will lead to such waters. Check with those in other states, too, and if necessary, plan a vacation that will take you to some of the best waters.

Some lakes and reservoirs have special management regulations such as length or slot limits that encourage the growth of larger crappie. These, in particular, are worth trying.

Fish Often, Year-round

Spawning season offers the best slab-hooking opportunities. Crappie move shallow then and are more easily found. Big egg-laden females weigh more than after spawning. However, savvy trophy hunters know big crappie can be taken year-round, and those who take trophy fish are consistently on the water many days year-round. Follow their example. Don't wait for perfect conditions. Get out there and fish.

Avoid Crowds

Barn-door crappie get cagey when people and boats are swarming. Fish when fewer folks are on the water—weekdays, in winter, at night. Better yet, fish fertile back country crappie waters that seldom see other anglers. These can often be found in wildlife management areas, national wildlife refuges and national forests. Many of them hold gigantic crappie, thanks to the lack of fishing pressure.

Watch for Isolated Underwater Cover

Larger crappie often use isolated underwater logs, treetops, etc. instead of visible cover pounded by more anglers. The hotspots usually are near (not necessarily in) deeper water, where big crappie can simply move deeper when feeling threatened.

The Northwest Factor

During prespawn periods, you'll have an advantage if you fish a lake's northwest section. Cold northerly winds blow over northwest banks, resulting in water that's as much as five degrees warmer there. This is highly attractive to big prespawn slabs.

Don't Blow a Chance

Don't lose the crappie of a lifetime because of avoidable problems: the line was frayed or too light for conditions, the hooks didn't hold, the drag was too loose or too tight, or the tackle was inadequate. Check often for fraying; cut and retie if necessary. Use the heaviest line suitable for conditions. Use premium hooks, always needle sharp. Always set your drag properly. Use quality poles, rods, reels and other tackle.

Be Different

Are other anglers zigging? Maybe you should zag. Fish become conditioned to certain baits, lures and presentations, and you may catch more lunkers by trying something unconventional—a rosy red minnow instead of a golden shiner, for example, or a new lure or presentation that hasn't caught on yet. Be open minded. Experiment.

Try Crankbaits

Although you may not catch as many fish, crappie taken on crankbaits average larger than fish taken on jigs or minnows. Also, because crankbaits are a little heavier than most other crappie baits, they can be cast farther with light tackle. This allows you to keep well away from the area you're fishing, a real advantage when targeting usually spooky trophies.

Pro Tip

"When vertical jigging standing timber, after your lure reaches the bottom, grab the line with your free hand and gently raise the lure bait up the tree. Crappie will not go down to hit your bait so raising the lure puts the bait in their face. They can't stand it"

--Kevin Rogers,
Crappie USA Classic qualifier six consecutive years

Play it Right

Crappie are called "papermouths" with good reason. It's easy to tear the hook from the mouth if you apply too much pressure. But you can lose a big crappie just as easily by applying too little pressure. Keep a tight line at all times, but don't play the fish too long or too hard.

Always Use a Landing Net

Bad things happen when you don't use a net: the fish thrashes off when you bend to grab it, or the hook rips out when you try swinging it in. A landing net is the best way to efficiently handle big crappie. Use one with a long handle that lets you stand while netting, giving an extra few feet of reach when you need it most.

Move Off Small Crappie

Small crappie are good practice subjects, but if you start catching lots of runts when targeting slabs, move somewhere else. The little guys are fun, but big ones aren't likely to be among them.

Try Shallower Water

In the situation just mentioned, most anglers will tend to move deeper. Deep water holds a greater mystique; we believe it's where the lunkers lurk. But that's not the case with crappie in most waters. When catching loads of small crappie, more often than not you'll find Mr. Big in shallower water, not deeper. Try it and see.

Don't Forget Hots pots

Remember the precise locations where you catch, lose or see big crappie—the specific stump, the particular bush, etc. A return visit could turn up the barn-door you missed, another trophy that moved in or a crappie that grew bigger after you released it. Use a good lake map or, better yet, a GPS unit, to mark hots pots in case memory fails.

Chapter VIII

CLEANING & COOKING CRAPPIE

How to Pan-Dress & Fillet Crappie

After the fun and excitement of crappie fishing has subsided, anglers must clean their catch. Two basic ways—filleting and pan-dressing—are used to prepare crappie for the table.

After the fish are cleaned, they can be cooked and eaten, or you can store the fillets or pan-dressed fish in the freezer until you're ready to prepare them. To avoid freezer burn and preserve freshness, it's best to immerse the prepared fish in water when you freeze them (either in zip-seal plastic freezer bags or plastic containers) or better yet, to vacuum-seal them using a product such as the Tilia FoodSaver. Be careful that the sharp fins on pan-dressed fish aren't positioned in such a way that they could puncture the wrapping or container.

How to Pan-Dress a Crappie

To pan-dress a crappie, you simply scrape away all the scales with a spoon or scaling tool, cut off the fish's head, remove the entrails, wash the fish thoroughly inside and out, and voila, you're finished. Leave the fins, tail and skin on. These are delicious in their own special ways and enhance the unsurpassed flavor of these popular panfish. You'll have to separate meat and bone as you eat pan-dressed fish, but many crappie connoisseurs believe this method of preparation produces a more tasty result.

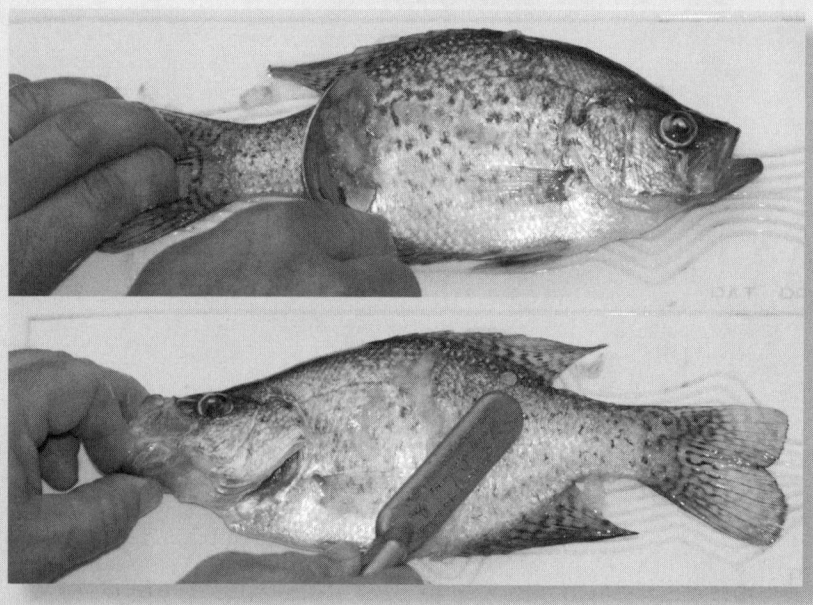

How to Fillet a Crappie

Filleting is a popular way to prepare crappie for cooking — simply cut the flesh away from the bones and skin. The result is a boneless piece of fish ready to be cooked. You will need a sharp fillet knife with a long, thin, flexible blade and a smooth cutting surface.

1. Lay the fish on a cutting board or other flat, hard surface. Grasping the fish's mouth, take the fillet knife and position it just behind the side (pectoral) fin. Slice downward to the backbone, keeping the rear of the knife blade up. Be careful not to cut into the fish's backbone.

2. Turn the knife blade toward the tail and continue cutting, staying on top of the back and belly fins. You'll feel resistance as you cut through the rib cage, but be careful not to cut into the backbone. It's better to cut too shallow than too deep. Continue your cut toward the tail, until you have almost, but not quite, cut the scaly fillet off.

3. With the fillet barely attached to the tail, flip it away from the fish. Position your knife on the narrow portion of the fillet and slice between the meat and the skin to remove the fillet. To obtain the maximum meat, cut very close to the skin. Flip the fish over and fillet the other side.

4. To finish, take each fillet, and with the tip of your fillet knife, carefully cut out the rib cage. To retrieve the most meat, angle your knife and slice close to the ribs. After you rinse the fillets, they're ready to cook or store.

Cleaning & Freezing Tips

- Beware of the sharp, spiny fins when cleaning crappie. They can cause nasty puncture wounds.
- Always cut away from you when dressing a fish. If the knife slips, then it's less likely to cut you.
- The common saying "A sharp knife is a safe knife" is true. The less you have to struggle or force the knife, the less likely the chance of an accident. For your safety, consider wearing a filleting glove, which protects your hands.
- The waste created from cleaning fish can get smelly if it has to sit for a while. Wrap the waste in newspaper and tape it securely, then store in your freezer until garbage day.
- You can extend freezer life of fish by several months if you soak the fish for 20 seconds in lemon juice. The ascorbic acid in lemon juice retards spoilage by slowing the growth of microorganisms and counteracting oxidation.

Crappie Recipes

The delicate white flesh of the crappie is delicious and easy to prepare. One of the crappie's greatest assets is its versatility. Serve it fried, smoked, poached, baked, broiled, braised, sautéed or barbecued. Or combine it with other foods for casseroles or chowders.

The most important rule in preparing crappie is never overcook it. Crappie is naturally tender and cooks quickly. It's done when it flakes easily when tested with a fork. Remember: the shorter the time from hook to cook, the better the flavor.

Buttermilk Batter Crappie Fillets

- 2 lbs. crappie fillets
- 4 eggs
- 1 cup buttermilk
- 1½ cups cracker meal
- ½ cup flour
- 1 tbsp. salt
- 1 tsp. black pepper
- Peanut oil

Beat the eggs until frothy, then add the buttermilk and mix. Dip fish fillets in this mixture, then roll in a mixture of the remaining four ingredients. Deep fry until golden-brown in peanut oil heated to 375°.

Pan-fried Crappie Dilly

- 6 crappie, pan-dressed
- 4 tbsp. butter
- 4 tbsp. fresh chopped dill
- ½ cup flour
- ½ cup cornmeal
- 1 tsp. salt
- 1 tsp. fresh-ground black pepper

Melt butter in a skillet and add dill. Dredge fish in a mixture of flour, cornmeal, salt and pepper. Sauté in dill butter until done.

Sautéed Crappie

- 10 crappie fillets
- 1 cup buttermilk
- 1½ cups Italian bread crumbs
- 1 tbsp. salt
- 1 tsp. freshly ground black pepper
- 4 tbsp. butter or margarine
- 2 tbsp. extra virgin olive oil

Soak the fish in buttermilk for 30 minutes. Remove and dredge in a mixture of the bread crumbs, salt and pepper. Fry the fillets in a combination of the butter and olive oil heated in a skillet. Add more butter and olive oil as needed. Fry until golden brown, or until the thickest part of the fish is easily flaked with a fork.

Tempura Crappie

- 1 cup all-purpose flour
- 1 cup cornstarch
- ¼ tsp. baking soda
- ¼ tsp. salt
- ⅛ tsp. black pepper
- 1 well-beaten egg
- 1½ cups water
- 2 lbs. crappie fillets, cut in serving-size pieces

Combine first five ingredients. Beat egg and water together, add the dry mix and stir until smooth. Dip fish fillets in batter, and deep-fry until golden-brown in peanut oil heated to 375°.

Crappie Stir-fry

1	lb. crappie fillets, cut in one-inch pieces
2	tbsp. sesame or peanut oil
2	carrots, thinly sliced
1	onion, thinly sliced
2	zucchini squash, thinly sliced
1	tsp. chopped parsley
¼	tsp. black pepper

In a wok or large skillet, heat oil, and add vegetables and thyme. Stir-fry until slightly tender. Season crappie fillets with pepper and add to the pan. Stir-fry until fish is opaque and flakes easily. Serve over a bed of hot rice.

Parmesan/Shrimp Crappie Bake

1	lb. crappie fillets
	White pepper
2	tbsp. butter
1	can cream of shrimp soup, undiluted
¼	cup grated Parmesan cheese
	Sweet paprika

Heat oven to 350°. Place a single layer of crappie fillets in a lightly buttered glass baking dish. Sprinkle with white pepper, and dot with butter. Pour soup over the fillets, and spread evenly. Sprinkle with Parmesan cheese and paprika. Bake, uncovered, for 20 minutes or until fish flakes easily when tested with a fork.

Crappie With Provençal Butter

2 eggs ¼ cup buttermilk 2 cloves garlic, minced ½ tsp. thyme ½ tsp. rosemary 4 crappie, pan-dressed	Beat the eggs until frothy, then add the buttermilk and mix. Dip fish fillets in this mixture, then roll in a mixture of the remaining four ingredients. Deep fry until golden-brown in peanut oil heated to 375°.

Cracker-Crumb Crappie

2 eggs 4 tbsp. evaporated milk 2 lbs. crappie fillets 1½ cups finely crushed Ritz crackers ½ cup flour Peanut oil for frying	Beat eggs until frothy, then add evaporated milk. Dip fish fillets in this mixture, then roll in a mixture of Ritz cracker crumbs and flour. Fry in peanut oil heated to 375°. Fish are done when they flake easily with a fork.

Mayo Crappie Bake

- 2 lbs. crappie fillets
- ½ cup mayonnaise
- 2 cups seasoned, dried bread crumbs

Coat crappie fillets with mayonnaise, and dredge in breadcrumbs. Arrange the fillets in a single layer in a well-greased glass baking dish or dishes. Bake at 450° for about 10 minutes or until fish flakes easily when tested with a fork.

Quick Grilled Crappie

- 1 lb. crappie fillets
- 2 tbsp. sugar
- 2 tbsp. paprika
- 1 tbsp. lemon pepper
- 2 tsp. fresh-ground black pepper
- 1 tsp. salt
- ¼ cup extra virgin olive oil

Sprinkle a mixture of the other ingredients on the fillets after lightly coating them with olive oil. Cover and allow to sit in the refrigerator while you fire up the grill. Lightly coat the grill or cooking grates with olive or canola oil to help keep the fish from sticking. Then grill each side for about two minutes until the fish begins to flake easily with a fork.

Special Occasion Crappie & Scallops Stew

1	medium onion, finely chopped
1	leek, white part only, thinly sliced
1	clove garlic, minced
1	tbsp. butter
2	cups chicken broth
2	medium tomatoes, peeled, seeded and diced
2	tbsp. fresh parsley, finely chopped
1	celery rib, finely chopped
1	bay leaf
¼	tsp. dried thyme
½	tsp. black pepper
1	cup dry white wine
1	lb. crappie fillets, cut into bite-sized pieces
½	lb. fresh scallops

Sauté the onion, leek and garlic in butter over low heat until soft. Transfer to a large stock pot, and add all other ingredients except the crappie and scallops. Mix well and bring to a boil. Reduce heat and simmer, covered, for 10 minutes.

Add crappie and scallops and cook until they turn opaque, 2 to 5 minutes. Serve in individual soup mugs garnished with chopped chives and croutons.

Southwestern Crappie Cakes with Chipotle Mayonnaise

- 1 tbsp. butter
- ½ cup onion, finely diced
- ¼ cup red bell pepper, finely diced
- ¼ cup fresh cilantro, chopped
- 1 lb. crappie fillets, cooked, flaked
- 1 tbsp. red pepper flakes
- 2 garlic cloves, minced
- 2 tbsp. flour
- 3 tbsp. dried bread crumbs
- ½ tsp. lemon pepper
- 3 tbsp. mayonnaise
- 2 egg whites, beaten
- Vegetable oil

Heat butter in a skillet over medium-high heat. Add onion and bell pepper and sauté 4 to 5 minutes. In a large bowl, add cilantro, fish, pepper flakes, garlic and cooled onion/pepper from pan. Sprinkle flour, breadcrumbs and lemon pepper over the mixture while you toss it, making sure to coat fish evenly. Fold in mayonnaise and egg whites. Form the mixture into 8 cakes about 3 inches in diameter. Add enough oil to just cover the bottom of a large skillet and heat over medium heat. When oil is hot, add cakes and cook, flipping once, until golden-brown on each side. Serve hot, topped with Chipotle Mayonnaise.

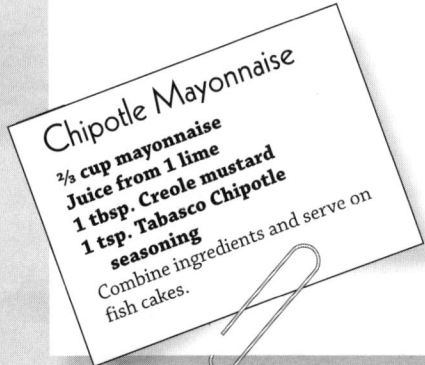

Chipotle Mayonnaise

- ⅔ cup mayonnaise
- Juice from 1 lime
- 1 tbsp. Creole mustard
- 1 tsp. Tabasco Chipotle seasoning

Combine ingredients and serve on fish cakes.

Poached Crappie Fillets with Shrimp Sauce

2 cups water
1 bay leaf
¼ tsp. salt
2 tbsp. lemon juice
8 to 12 crappie fillets

SHRIMP SAUCE:
2 tbsp. butter or margarine
2 tbsp. flour
Pinch white pepper
½ tsp. salt
Dash paprika
1 cup milk
1 tsp. Worcestershire sauce
½ cup diced, cooked shrimp

In a 10-inch skillet, combine water, bay leaf, ¼ teaspoon salt and the lemon juice. Bring to a boil over medium-high heat. Add fillets. Reduce heat to low. Simmer, covered, for 3 to 5 minutes, or until fish is firm and opaque and just begins to flake. Drain and discard poaching liquid. Cover fish to keep warm. Set aside.

To prepare the sauce, melt the butter in an 8-inch skillet over low heat. Add the flour, white pepper, salt and paprika, and stir until blended. Add the milk slowly, stirring constantly and taking care not to scorch the mixture. Cook, stirring, until smooth and thickened. Add the Worcestershire sauce and shrimp, stir and heat through. Serve the shrimp sauce over the fillets. Garnish with a light sprinkling of paprika and snipped fresh chives or parsley.

Savory Fried Crappie

6 crappie fillets
1 large lemon, cut in half
1 tbsp. olive oil
½ tsp. black pepper
1 egg, well beaten
½ tsp. dry mustard
Yellow cornmeal

Place fillets in a bowl and squeeze the lemon over the fish. Be sure each piece is thoroughly coated with juice. Pour olive oil over fish, add the black pepper and egg, and work both well into the fillets. Add the dry mustard, and mix it into the other ingredients, tumbling the fish over with your hands until the seasonings are about equally blended. Set the bowl in the refrigerator and allow to chill 30 minutes. When you're ready to fry the fish, remove the fillets from the bowl one at a time and dredge in corn meal. Use your fingers to knead the corn meal onto each fillet. Coat them well. Drop the fillets in hot peanut oil immediately as they are coated. Fry until golden brown.

Index

Advanced Crappie Secrets (book), 66
Arkansas Game & Fish Commission, 127-29
Baitfish, 17, 38, 55
   gizzard shad , 37, 75
   goldfish, 75-76
   shad, 74
   sunfish fry, 74
   threadfin shad, 16-17, 37, 75
Bass Research Foundation, Twin Lakes Chapter, 127-29
Beaver Lake, Arkansas, 10, 13
Bill Lewis Lures, Alexandria, Louisiana, 52
Black Crappie (*Pomoxis nigromaculatus*), 8-11
   in California, 9
   in Idaho, 9
   in Oregon, 9
   range of, 9
   in the United States, 9
   in Washington State, 9
Black River, Arkansas , 82
Blacknose crappie, 13
Bladebaits, 32 , 58, 133
   adjustment to, 63
   characteristics of, 9, 59
   color of, 59, 63
   fishing techniques with, 59-60, 63
   hooks for, 63
   rigs for, 63
   size of, 60
   vertical jigging with, 60
   vibration of, 63
Bland, Billy, 72
Bobbers, 39-40
   slip, 40, 68
   fixed, 40
   cigar float, 68
Bob Kidd Lake, Arkansas, 129
Brush piles
   brush piles and crappie, 129-130, 167
   cedar, 119-120
   fishing techniques for, 130 , 131
Bull Shoals Lake, Arkansas, 13, 127-129
Bull Shoals/Norfork Fish Cover Project, 127, 129
Calico bass, (See black crappie)
Campbell, Alexander, 11
Chicot Lake, Arkansas, 129
Crankbaits, 48, 93-94, 99, 169, 170, 174
   colors of , 49
   deep-diving, 49, 55
   fishing points with, 94
   fishing techniques, 49
   lipless, 51-52, 55, 133
   mini, 32
   rods for, 55
   top-running crappie and, 50
   trolling, 55
   vegetation and, 55
   vibrating, 52
Crappie
   alternate names for, 11
   beaver lodges and, 15
   color change in males, 12
   cover and, 13, 15, 97
   in creek channels, 53
   fish shelters and, 15
   fishing tactics, 87-91
   fishing techniques for, 6, 15-19, 53-54, 88-89, 108, 116, 129, 134-135, 144-147, 162
   food habits, 10
   location of, 14-16, 94-95, 134
   nesting behavior of, 12, 80, 88-89
   range of, 9
   reproduction of, 12
   scents and, 119
   seasonal habits of, 12-13
   size range of, 9-10
   spawning behavior of, 12, 53, 81-82, 84, 86-87, 89, 95
   surface feeding behavior of, 107
   thermoclines and, 98, 110
   water depth and, 81, 95
   water temperature and , 53, 80
   weather and, 92-93, 134
   world record for, 10

Crappie pros, 23, 80, 135, 145, 163, 174
Crappie USA Classic Tournament, 166
Crapet (Canadian-French term), 11
Cooking and preparation
   (See also Recipes)
   cleaning, 175, 181
   filleting, 180, 181
   freezing, 181
   pan-dressing, 175, 178-179
Cypress trees, 17, 107-108, 145
Dagmar Wildlife Management Area, Arkansas, 129
DeQueen Lake, Arkansas, 129
Dierks Lake, Arkansas, 129
Docks, 145, 163
Dragling, 160-161
Elmdale Lake, Arkansas, 129
Enid Lake, Mississippi, 10
Fall crappie fishing
   fishing techniques, 112-113, 115-116
   location of fish, 116
   structure and, 114-116
   vertical structure and, 114
Fall turnover, 110, 112, 113
   in lakes, 110, 112-113
   lures for, 114,-115
   in rivers, 115-116
Filipek, Steve, 72
Fish attractors
   christmas tree, 130
   man-made, 125
Fletcher, Bill, 129-131
GPS, 134-135
Hinkle Lake, Arkansas, 129
Hole fishing techniques, 154-155, 158-159
Hooks, 33
Huckabee, Todd, 166-171
Huffman, Tim, 23
Hybrid crappie, 10, 12
International Game Fish Association, 10
Inundated small ponds and lakes, 16
Jigs, 31, 34, 36-39, 53, 85
   bait and, 42
   jig/minnow combinations, 42
   rigs for, 42
   scent on, 42
   techniques, 91
   weedless, 40
Jonesboro, Arkansas, 82
Kentucky Department of Fish and Wildlife Resources, 126
Kerr Lake, Virginia, 10
Knots,
   Palomar, 30
   trilene, 31
Lake Barkley, Kentucky,
   brush pile study on, 126-127
Lake Elizabeth, Wisconsin, 10
Live baits
   catalpa worms, 77
   cockroaches, 76
   crawfish, 77
   crickets, 76
   damselfly larvae, 77
   dragonfly larvae, 77
   earthworms, 76
   freshwater shrimp, 76
   grasshoppers , 77
   maggots, 77
   mayfly larvae, 77
   scuds, 77
   wasp larvae, 77
Lures, 31, 90, 168, 171
   colors of, 36, 85
   presentation of, 85
   selection of, 36-39
   size, 36
McCadams, Steve, 163
McClintock, Guy, 28, 136, 138
Marshall, Wally, 135, 145
Minnows
   blacknose dace, 67
   bluntnose , 67
   care of, 67-71
   common, 67
   creek chub, 67
   Cyprinidae, 64, 66

fathead, 66
   fishing techniques with, 70-71
   golden shiner, 64, 66
   hooking, 71
   hooks for, 71
   hornyhead chub, 67
   as invasive species, 67
   minnow buckets and, 66
   mudminnows, 67
   red shiner, 67
   rigs for, 71
   rosy red, 72
Mississippi River, 143, 136
Moore, Curt, 154-159
Moore, W.T., 154-159
Mountain Home, Arkansas, 129
Mountain View, Arkansas, 155
National Fresh Water Fishing Hall of Fame, 10
New Techniques That Catch More Crappie (book), 81
Night fishing
   baits, 105
   crappie nighttime behavior, 102
   depth of fish, 104
   hooks for, 104
   in lakes, 101
   lights for, 103-104
   rigs for, 104-105
   tactics, 100-104
   techniques, 100-102, 104-105
Norfork Lake, Arkansas, 127, 129-130
Oklahoma City, Oklahoma, 166
Otoe County, Nebraska, 10
Oxbows, 136, 138, 148, 153
Peace, Bill, 82-86
Peeler, Lewis, 143-147
Perry, Buck, 142
Poles
   cane, 20
   crappie poles, 23
   fiberglass, 22
   jigging, 20, 22
   types of, 23
Pro fishing tips, 135, 163, 174
River channels, 98
River fishing tactics, 82-86
Recipes, 182
   Buttermilk Batter Crappie Fillets, 183
   Chipotle Mayonnaise, 189
   Cracker-Crumb Crappie, 186
   Crappie Stir-fry, 185
   Crappie With Provençal Butter, 186
   Mayo Crappie Bake, 187
   Pan-fried Crappie Dilly, 183
   Parmesan/Shrimp Crappie Bake, 185
   Poached Crappie Fillets with Shrimp Sauce, 190
   Quick Grilled Crappie, 187
   Sautéed Crappie, 184
   Savory Fried Crappie, 191
   Southwestern Crappie Cakes with Chipotle Mayonnaise, 189
   Special Occasion Crappie & Scallops Stew, 188
   Tempura Crappie, 184
Reels
   baitcasting, 26
   maintenance of, 27
   spincasting, 26
   spinning, 26
   use of, 27
Rods, 24, 168
   action, 24-25
   characteristics of, 25
   maintenance of, 25
   material, 26
   power rating of, 24-25
   selection of, 26
   spincasting, 20
   spinning, 20
   use of, 25
Rogers, Kevin, 80, 174
St. Francis River, Arkansas, 82
Seasonal fishing considerations, 81-84
Sight fishing
   locations for, 89-90

techniques, 87-90
Sling-shotting, 161-162
Spinners, 99
   fishing techniques with, 44-47
   horsehead, 32, 45, 47
   safety-pin, 32, 44-45, 47
   weighted (in-line), 45, 46, 47
Spoons, 56, 99
   casting with, 56-57
   changing hooks on, 58
   fishing techniques with, 57-58
   jigging with, 57-58
   rigging, 58
   trolling with, 56-57
   weedless, 58
Spring crappie fishing, 87-88
   fishing tactics, 92
   spawning season and, 78, 80
Structure, 102, 142-144, 145-147
Stump-knocking, 161
Sugarloaf Lake, Arkansas, 129
Summer crappie fishing, 170-171
   baits, 107
   bottom fishing during, 106-107
   crankbaits and, 49-50
   crappie behavior during, 102-103
   fishing tactics, 96-99, 106-107
   movement of fish during, 103
   storm fronts and, 108-109
Sunfish Centrarchidae, 8
Sunrise-Sunset tables, 81
Superstructure, 143, 144
Table Rock Lake, Missouri, 81
Tackle, 20, 28-29, 33
Tackle boxes and bags, 29, 33
Tailspinners, 32, 58 -61
Taylor, Arkansas, 72
Tennessee Valley Authority, 127
Tennessee Wildlife Resources Agency, 126
Terminal Tackle, 30
   hooks, 30
   line, 30
   weights, 30
Thicket structures, 18
Trolling
   baits for, 139, 140
   boats for, 139
   crappie and, 136, 138
   equipment for, 138, 139
   jigs and, 118
   lures for, 139
   rigs, 138-139
   side-trolling, 108
   techniques, 138-141
Trophy tactics, 80-81, 164, 166-175
   144, 166
U.S. Army Corps of Engineers, 127-130, 144, 166
Uncle Guy (See McClintock, Guy)
Underwater humps, 18-19
Vasey, Dr. Fred, 81
Vertical jigging, 53, 133
   presentation, 53
   sunken timber and, 53
   suspended summer and winter crappie and, 53
   techniques, 53
Weiss Lake, Alabama, 12
Westwego Canal, Louisiana, 10
White Crappie (*Pomoxis annularis*), 8
White crappie, 9
   range of, 9
   size of, 10
   world record, 9
White River, Arkansas, 82
Winter fishing
   bank fishing, 134
   fishing techniques, 121-124
   lures for, 123
   rigs for, 121-124
   structure and, 125-126
   tackle for winter, 121-122
   underwater springs and, 133
Wunderle, Steve, 66, 81
Wynne, Arkansas, 143
Zebco reels, 168